LIVING
ENGLISH STRUCTURE
FOR SCHOOLS

LIVING
ENGLISH STRUCTURE
FOR SCHOOLS

By

W. STANNARD ALLEN, B.A. (LOND.)

Illustrated by

ROY DAVIS

LONGMAN

LONGMAN GROUP LIMITED
London

*Associated companies, branches and representatives
throughout the world*

First published 1958
New impressions *1959; *1960; *1962 (twice); *1963;
*1964 (twice); *1965 (twice); *1966; *1967;
*1968; *1969; *1970; *1971 (twice);
*1972 (twice);
*1973; *1974

ISBN 0 582 52102 5

Printed in Hong Kong by
Sheck Wah Tong Printing Press

INTRODUCTION

THE original edition of *Living English Structure* was designed for use in evening classes of adult learners. Its wealth of exercises caused many teachers to introduce it also into schools, where they found that although the general scheme of the book was very useful, many of the sentences that were suitable for older students were not suitable for pupils in schools. On a recent visit to Jordan and the Lebanon the author was happy to meet many teachers who were using the book in schools and finding it less satisfactory than with older students. The direct result of the critical comments of these teachers is the present book, a special school version of *Living English Structure*.

It differs from the original version in the following respects.

1. The subject-matter of the exercises is made suitable for younger pupils.
2. The notes to the exercises are entirely rewritten and are much fuller.
3. Many new exercises have been devised for this special school edition.
4. The key is not included with the book, but can be obtained separately.
5. An up-to-date appendix on clauses (and the conjunctions introducing them) has been added.

The original Advanced sections have been omitted, and only a few exercises are listed as Advanced. The Elementary and Intermediate gradings do not refer so much to vocabulary as to the nature of the grammatical and structural points involved in the exercise. These terms are only rough guides; some schools have as many as eight or more English lessons a week, in other countries three or four is the rule. Some languages do not use the Roman alphabet, so that pupils spend a longer time learning to read after they have acquired a mastery of some elementary spoken English. For this reason it is not possible to recommend at which stage Intermediate exercises become more appropriate than those marked Elementary, but the intelligent teacher will soon see when the standard becomes too difficult for his own pupils.

This book offers an essentially practical survey and revision of grammatical material up to and slightly beyond the standard of the overseas equivalents of the General Certificate of Education examination, " Ordinary " Level. The very concise but thorough treatment of clauses and their associated conjunctions in the appendix will, it is hoped, be a valuable introduction to all kinds of composition work that will be practised in the year preceding such an examination. The exercises can lead up to and be used in conjunction with any suitable book for vocabulary building and composition.

The author is very grateful for the many critical comments and suggestions that he has received concerning the original *Living English Structure*. Especial thanks are due to Mr. Ralph Cooke and members of the teaching staff at Davies's School of English, London, who compiled an invaluable list of suggestions at the time this present book was on the stocks; and Mr. Cooke was good enough to read the manuscript and offer further critical comments in time for them to be incorporated in this first edition. It is hoped that this School Version will solve the problems of those teachers who have wanted something similar for pupils in schools, and will also be of use to those who want a shorter book of exercises and grammatical notes for general teaching purposes.

W. S. ALLEN

Istanbul,
February 1958

SOME USEFUL BOOKS ON THIS SUBJECT FOR TEACHERS

Jespersen: *Essentials of English Grammar* (Allen and Unwin)
Palmer: *A Grammar of English Words* (Longmans)
Hornby and Gatenby: *Advanced Learner's Dictionary* (Oxford)
Zandvoort: *A Handbook of English Grammar* (Longmans)
Partridge: *Usage and Abusage* (Hamish Hamilton)
Vallins: *The Pattern of English* (Deutsch)
Fowler: *A Dictionary of Modern English Usage* (Oxford)
Hornby: *A Guide to Patterns and Usage* (Oxford)
Cooke: *Notes on Learning English* (Longmans)

CONTENTS

NOUNS AND ARTICLES

EXERCISE 1. Elementary

Note: Things that we can count may take "a" or "an" in the singular. We call this the Indefinite Article.

Examples: a book, books; an egg, eggs.

Things that we cannot count may not take the indefinite article, and for the same reason there is usually no plural form of such nouns.

Examples: flour, ink, honesty.

Make these sentences plural:

1. A dog is an animal.
2. A potato is a vegetable.
3. A student is not always good.
4. A chair is made of wood.
5. A boy likes a game.
6. A pencil is like a pen.
7. An eye is blue or brown.
8. A fish can swim.
9. A cow gives milk.
10. A picture is pretty.
11. We can read a book.
12. A garden has a tree.
13. We drink tea out of a cup.
14. An apple grows on a tree.
15. A mother is kind to a little child.
16. A girl likes a sweet.
17. A teacher is a man or a woman.
18. A fly is an insect.
19. A dog hates a cat.
20. A box has a lid.
21. A chicken is a bird.

22. A cat eats meat.
23. We can make a cake with flour, milk and an egg.
24. We fill our pen with ink.
25. A writer writes a book.

EXERCISE 2.   Elementary

Make these sentences singular, using the Indefinite Article:

1. Horses are animals.
2. Balls are toys.
3. Bullocks are useful animals.
4. Boots are kinds of shoes.
5. Watches are small clocks.
6. Farmers use ploughs.
7. Roses are beautiful flowers.
8. Frenchmen are Europeans.
9. Girls wear dresses.
10. Children are not always good.
11. There are always tables and chairs in dining-rooms.
12. Long sentences are hard for beginners.
13. Hungry boys eat large dinners.

No. 13

14. Ants are insects.
15. Soldiers are brave men.
16. Coats have collars.
17. Nouns are words.
18. Houses have roofs.
19. Postmen wear caps.

20. Oranges are good to eat.
21. Classrooms have blackboards.
22. Dogs are good friends to men.
23. Pounds buy more than pence.
24. Cities are big towns.
25. Schools are large buildings.

EXERCISE 3. Elementary

Note: In this exercise do not forget that the Indefinite Article ("a" or "an") will not be used with things that you cannot count.

Add "a" or "an" where necessary:

1. ... cigarette is made of ... tobacco and ... paper.
2. ... milk comes from ... cow.
3. We make ... butter and ... cheese from ... milk.
4. ... window is made of ... glass.
5. ... handkerchief is made of ... piece of cloth.
6. ... grass always grows in ... English field.
7. ... chair is made of ... wood.
8. ... cat has ... tail.
9. ... cat eats ... meat.
10. ... ring is made of ... gold or silver.
11. ... coffee is ... drink.
12. ... coat is made of ... wool.
13. ... fish swims in ... water.
14. We can write ... letter on ... paper.
15. ... piano makes ... music.
16. ... iron is metal.
17. ... bread is made from ... flour, and ... flour is made from ... wheat.
18. ... orange grows on ... tree.
19. ... child must have ... food.
20. ... sugar is nice in ... cup of tea.
21. We eat ... soup with ... spoon.
22. ... knife is made of ... metal.
23. ... cow eats ... grass in ... summer.

24. I like ... jam on ... piece of ... bread.
25. I can write ... letter in ... ink or with ... pencil.

EXERCISE 4.   Elementary

Note: The Indefinite Article can have two kinds of plural:
(*a*) no word at all.   (*b*) Some (any).

(*a*) This is a general plural.
    A horse (=one): horses (=all).   Horses are animals.
(*b*) This is used for a small or indefinite number.
    They have two cows and some horses.
    Here are some sentences for your homework.

(The word "some" changes to "any" in negative sentences and sometimes in questions.   A later exercise practises this.)

"Some" is used in the same way before an uncountable noun to express the idea of a small or indefinite quantity.

    Bread is good for us.   (All bread; bread in general.)
    Give me some bread.   (A small quantity.)

Add "a", "an" or "some" where necessary:

1. ... table has four legs.
2. We can write on ... paper or on ... blackboard.
3. ... apple has ... sweet taste.
4. ... fruit is very good to eat.
5. Please give me ... milk.
6. There is ... dirt on this plate and ... dirty mark on the tablecloth.
7. ... man gave me ... books this morning.
8. ... good pupil is never late for ... lesson.
9. ... book about ... philosophy is not good for ... child.
10. Put ... lemon in your soup instead of ... salt.
11. I want ... glass of ... lemonade with ... sugar in it.
12. ... bed made of ... iron is better than one made of ... wood.
13. ... Australian sheep gives us ... very good wool.
14. You must write in ... ink; here is ... pen.
15. Give me ... ink to write ... letter.

16. Do you take ... sugar in ... tea?
17. ... garden usually has ... flowers in it.
18. I like ... music very much.
19. ... house made of ... stone can be very pretty.
20. There is ... pencil and ... writing-paper.

EXERCISE 5. Intermediate

Note: Names of things we can count (countable nouns) **may** take the Indefinite Article.

Names of things we cannot count (uncountable nouns) do not take the Indefinite Article; and, as they cannot be counted, they can very rarely have a plural form.

But some nouns have more than one meaning, or the meaning can change in different sentences; it is possible for some nouns to be both countable and uncountable.

> This table is made of wood. (=substance.)
> There is a wood near the river. (=a small forest.)
> A window is made of glass. (=substance.)
> Pour the water into a glass. (=a thing for drinking out of.)
> Give him a boiled egg. (=one whole egg.)
> There is some egg on your coat. (=a small quantity of the substance.)

(a) *Say which of the following words can take an Indefinite Article, i.e. which ones are countable nouns.*

(b) *Say which of these words can be either countable or uncountable nouns; make short sentences with these in both senses:*

air	dirt	literature
book	mountain	camel
beef	dress	music
shop	fish	poetry
butter	grass	poem
apple	breath	sand
cheese	friend	sun
clothing	friendship	sunshine
coat	hair	sleep
coffee	ice	smoke
darkness	storm	iron

EXERCISE 6.   Elementary and Intermediate

Note: Notice that when we want to introduce an indefinite subject in English, we do so with *"There is"*, etc. We do not say:

        A chair is in the corner.

but   There is a chair in the corner.   Similarly:

        There will be some money for you tomorrow.

        There were some fine palm-trees in the park.

The *Definite Article* "the" is used before a noun that is already known to us, either because it has already been mentioned, or because our commonsense tells us which particular one (or ones) the writer or speaker has in mind.

    Examples: (*a*)   A man was walking across a field with a dog. The dog's name was Spot and the man was his master.

              (*b*)   The sun is hot today.

              (*c*)   Please meet me at the station.

Add "a", "an", "some", or "the" where necessary:

1.   ... children love ... fruit.
2.   It is pleasant to read ... book in ... afternoon.
3.   ... books are interesting for ... child.
4.   There is ... garden behind ... house.
5.   I have ... pen and ... pencil.
6.   ... tea is very hot, I must put ... milk in it.
7.   ... postman has just put ... letter under ... door.
8.   You must give him ... food and ... cup of coffee.
9.   ... door of ... garage is broken.
10.   There are ... beautiful flowers in ... park.
11.   I want ... glass of ... milk.
12.   ... student at ... back of ... class is reading ... newspaper.
13.   It is not good to smoke ... cigarette before ... meal.
14.   ... page of ... book is torn.
15.   There is ... fly in ... lemonade.
16.   ... luggage is on ... platform.
17.   ... butcher opposite ... library always sells ... good meat.
18.   ... cat may look at ... king.
19.   ... donkeys are ... stupid animals.

20. Put ... butter on ... potatoes.
21. I am fond of ... apples with ... cheese.
22. He always smokes ... cigarette with ... cup of ...coffee.
23. Take ... umbrella with you to ... office, it may rain.
24. ... car is ready now.
25. I want ... tin of ... peaches, ... sugar, and ... pound of ... raspberry jam.

Section 2

ELEMENTARY NEGATIVES AND QUESTIONS

EXERCISE 7.   Elementary

Note: The verb *"to be"* and all the Helping Verbs normally make questions by inversion with the subject, and negatives by adding *"not"*.

Make the following statements (a) negative, (b) questions:

1. He can read English.
2. She has a brother.
3. I must do it now.
4. He is very late.
5. They have time to do it.
6. You can wait here.
7. I am right.
8. We can see from here.
9. He must eat it.
10. They are French.
11. You must tell him everything.
12. He can leave now.
13. You have a knife.
14. She can put it on the table.
15. I must keep it.
16. I am early.
17. They can go now.
18. You must write to her.
19. He has a good one.
20. I can come tomorrow.

EXERCISE 8.   Elementary

Note: All ordinary full verbs require the verb *"to do"* in order to make their negative and question forms. The sentences in this exercise are all in the General or Habitual Present tense (Simple Present: see Exercises 46 to 49).

Make the following statements (a) negative, (b) questions:

1. John likes tea.
2. He sells good cakes.
3. You speak softly.
4. It tastes good.
5. I read well.
6. He takes English lessons.
7. They often go to the pictures.
8. It costs a pound.
9. She swims well.
10. They try to understand.
11. He walks to work.
12. I do it well.
13. You sleep well.
14. They play football.
15. He knows Arabic.
16. We believe him.
17. I keep it in my pocket.
18. You write to them every day.
19. He lives in this house.
20. She feels well.

Section 3

POSSESSIVES

EXERCISE 9.   Elementary

Note: The answer to the question *"Whose?"* is given by the pairs of words: my/mine; your/yours; his/his; her/hers; our/ours; your/yours; their/theirs.

The first of each pair of words is the form we use before a noun: *This is my/your etc. book.*

The second word is the form we use without a following noun: *This (book) is mine/yours etc.*

Notice that only *"his"* has the same form for both positions; and that *"its"* (for things) is used only *before* a noun and cannot stand alone.

ALL BOOKS TO BE SHUT FOR THIS EXERCISE. THE TEACHER ASKS QUESTIONS ON THE FOLLOWING PATTERNS:

(a) Is this my, your, her etc. ... paper, book, pupil, room etc.? ...

(b) Is this book, coat, parcel etc. ... mine, yours, hers etc.? ...

(*c*) This isn't my, your etc. ... paper, book etc., is it?
(*No, it isn't your, my etc., ... paper etc., it's mine etc.*)
(*d*) Whose is this? Whose pen, book etc. is this (that)?
(*e*) Mix the above types of question.

EXERCISE 10. Intermediate

Note: Another useful kind of possessive is the type *"a friend of mine/yours etc.",* which is another way of saying *"one of my/your etc. friends".*

Complete these sentences with suitable possessives:

1. This doesn't look like ... book; it must be ...
    (*Use many different forms in this one.*)
2. Tell him not to forget ... homework; she mustn't forget ..., either.
3. "Tell me, isn't that ... English teacher over there?"
    "Oh no, that's ... History teacher."
4. Have you done ... homework? I've finished ...

No. 4

5. It was a good idea of ... to put ... books with ...
6. Su'ad and Ismat have forgotten ... notebooks again; Tom and Bill have forgotten ..., too.
7. George has lost ... pencil; perhaps you can lend him ...
8. I met a friend of ... at a party last night.
9. Who bought these oranges? ... is a very dry one; what's ... like?

10. She wonders if you have seen a book of ... lying about somewhere.
11. You can take ... ticket and give me ...
12. John is coming here next week; ... father and ... were school friends.
13. They asked me to call on a friend of ... in London.
14. He introduced me to a neighbour of ...
15. We've taken ... share; has she taken ...?

Section 4

ADVERB ORDER

EXERCISE 11. Elementary and Intermediate

Note: A great number of adverbs tell us one of three things about the verb:

1. **How** the action took place (Manner): *quickly, well, in ink.*
2. **Where** the action took place (Place): *here, outside, at home.*
3. **When** the action took place (Time): *today, then, last year.*

In a normal sentence these adverbs would appear in this same order:

Example: He spoke well at the debate this morning.

The adverb of time can also come at the beginning of a sentence instead of at the end. This gives it a little more emphasis, but is a good place to put it if we want to avoid a long tail of adverbs.

With verbs of movement the adverb of place (or direction) becomes a kind of object, and so comes immediately after the verb, before any adverbs of manner.

Example: He went to the station by taxi.

It is usual to put more exact expressions before more general ones.

Example: He was born at six o'clock on a cold December morning in the year 1850.

Put the given adverbs in their correct places:

1. She went (to school, at 10 o'clock).
2. He was born (in the year 1923, at 10 a.m., on June 14th).

3. She drinks coffee (every morning, at home).
4. Our teacher spoke to us (in class, very rudely, this morning).
5. I saw my friend off (at 7 o'clock, at the station, this morning).
6. He worked for our cause (all his life, passionately).
7. My father was working (at his office, very hard, all day yesterday).
8. My sister speaks English (very well); but she writes French (badly).
9. They stayed (all day, quietly, there).
10. I like coffee (in the morning, very much).
11. The train arrived (this morning, late).
12. He played (at the Town Hall, last night, beautifully, in the concert).
13. I shall meet you (outside your office, tomorrow, at 2 o'clock).
14. We are going (for a week, to Switzerland, on Saturday).
15. Let's go (tonight, to the pictures).

Section 5

PRONOUNS

EXERCISE 12.   Elementary

Note: **Verbs with two objects** (person and thing).

If the person is a pronoun, it will normally precede the *Direct Object.*

I told a story to my friend.

I told him a story.

This last sentence shows the usual pattern for this kind of verb; the first sentence shows the word-order we use when the indirect object is of special interest to the speaker.

Notice that whenever the *Indirect Object* precedes the *Direct Object*, the preposition ("to" or "for") is omitted. A very few verbs, the most important of which are "say" and "explain" always keep the preposition "to" and the word-order Direct Object plus Indirect Object if these are simple nouns or pronouns:

"Will you explain this problem to me?"

"I said good-morning to George."

This word-order is changed whenever the Direct Object seems to be long and weighty (a long phrase or clause, for example).

"Will you explain to me how to do this problem?"

"I said to George, 'Please come in and sit down'."

Replace the expressions in bold type by pronouns:

1. John gave the book to **Henry.**
2. **Jane** bought some sweets for **her mother.**
3. Explain **the answer** to **the student.**
4. **My sister and I** told **my little brother** a story.
5. **Alec and Mary** gave a box of chocolates to **my sister and me.**
6. **You and I** must give a present to **John.**
7. **John** will find her coat for **Mary.**
8. **Henry and Alec** came to see **me and my wife.**
9. Give this one to **the baby.**
10. **My friend and I** told **John** about **our journey** last week.

EXERCISE 13. Intermediate

Note: **Case.**

1. After "between" and "let" the objective case is used.

Let him play the first game.

Come and sit between John and me.

2. If a pronoun is not felt to be the active or real subject of a sentence, the natural form to use is the objective case. This is never felt to be an object, but is merely the form used for a pronoun that stands isolated in some way from a verb it might be the subject of. (Compare the French "C'est moi".)

That's him over there.

Don't disturb yourself, it's only me.

If I were her, I'd write a letter about it.

(*Showing a photo*) . . . and this is me standing by the fountain.

If a relative clause follows this predicative use of a pronoun, the pronoun may be in either the subjective or objective case to agree with the relative pronoun.

> It was she who told you, wasn't it? (She told you.)
>
> It was her you meant, wasn't it?   (You meant her.)

3. The words "than" and "as" are conjunctions and so may be followed by either case.

> I like you more than she (does).
>
> I like you more than her (=than I like her).
>
> I saw her as clearly as he (did).
>
> I saw her as clearly as him (=as I saw him).

In practice (especially in Spoken English) the objective case is often used where we should logically expect the subjective. This is now accepted in speech, but not in writing. With **transitive verbs** (as above) there is clearly a danger of misunderstanding; with **intransitive verbs** the meaning is always quite clear whatever case is used. Students should notice that the objective case is usual whenever the pronoun is further qualified (for example, by adding "*both*" or "*all*").

> You're cleverer than them all.
>
> You're much taller than me, but she's taller than us all.

Choose the correct pronoun in these sentences:

1. They knew all about my friend and (I me).
2. Basil gave Harry and (I me) an ice-cream, and then we went to the pictures with (he him) and his friend.
3. He told Mary and (me I) to go with (he him) and his mother.
4. What would you do if you were (he him)?
5. Let you and (me I) be friends!
6. We're much stronger than (they them) at football.
7. Just between you and (me I) it's (him he) I'm afraid of, not (she her).
8. I know you're bigger than (I me), in fact you're bigger than (we us) both, but we're not afraid of you.
9. It was (he him) I was talking about.
10. Well, let's pretend for a moment! I'll be (her she) and you be (I me). Now imagine there's a quarrel between (her she) and (I me). How would you settle it?

Section 6

POSSESSIVE CASE

EXERCISE 14. Elementary and Intermediate

Note: The possessive case (sometimes called the Saxon Genitive) is normally used with living creatures and proper names only:

> a boy's name, a king's palace, a spider's web.

Plurals in "s" do not add another "s" but in writing we place the apostrophe last:

> the boys' caps, horses' legs; *but* the men's work.

> (The irregular plurals "mice" and "lice" have no possessive.)

The commoner names ending in "s" usually add 's (pronounced as a separate syllable):

> Saint James's Park [dʒeimziz], Mr. Jones's house, Charles's coat, Keats's poetry. (Keats, not being such a normal name, sometimes behaves as in the next paragraph.)

Less usual names are more often treated like the plurals above; classical and mythological names are nearly always treated in this way:

> Keats' poetry, Pears' soap, Archimedes' screw.

(In general, we use 's where we can, unless it is clumsy to pronounce.)

Compound names or group names have the possessive on the last part only:

> my father-in-law's house, Romeo and Juliet's love.

> Sinbad the Sailor's adventures, Brown the baker's daughter.

> (But Mary, the baker's daughter; Henry's and Mary's books, or Henry's books and Mary's.)

A certain number of idioms, especially of time and measure, have a possessive form:

> in a week's time, three days' holiday, at my wit's end, out of harm's way, a shilling's worth.

Put into the possessive form:

The coat of the boy.	The plays of Beaumont and Fletcher.
The clothes of the boys.	The hats of ladies.
The father of James.	The music of Strauss.
The names of the women.	The typist of Mr. Sims.

The tail of the fox. She's done the work of a whole day.
The glass of someone else. In the time of a week or two.
The poems of Bridges. The parents of all the other boys.
The poems of Byron and The house of Henry and Mr. Jones.
   Tennyson. During the holiday of two weeks of
The palace of St. James. my friend Ahmed.

Here is a traditional children's puzzle:

The son of Pharaoh's daughter was the daughter of Pharaoh's son.

Section 7

INTRODUCTION TO INTERROGATIVES

EXERCISE 15. Elementary

Note: WHO? Pronoun for persons only.
   WHAT? (*a*) Pronoun for things in general.
      (*b*) Adjective for persons or things in general.
   WHICH? (*a*) Pronoun for things from a limited group.
      (*b*) Adjective for persons or things from a limited group.

Who wrote "Hamlet"?
What is your name?
What time is it? *What* dramatist wrote Hamlet?
Which is yours—this one or that?
Which book is yours? *Which* boy here knows the answer?
(See also Exercises 102 to 106.)

Add a question-word to the following questions:

1. .... is your name?
2. .... is that pretty girl?
3. .... is your telephone number?
4.   Here are the books! ..... is yours?
5. .... is coming to tea?
6. .... trees grow in Egypt?
7. .... is yours, the orange or the banana?

8. *What* colour is it?
9. *who* makes your shoes?
10. *who* makes tea sweet?
11. *who* wants a piece of bread?
12. *Which* piece of bread is yours?
13. *what* is the name of your baker?
14. *which* is his shop, the one at the end of the road, or the one near the Post Office?
15. *who* understands this exercise?
16. *which* of you understand this exercise?
17. *what* is the answer to my question?
18. *who* knows the answer?
19. *who* teaches you English?
20. *what* are you learning now?

Section 8

TELLING THE TIME

EXERCISE 16.   Elementary and Intermediate

Note: The usual (informal) way of reading the time between 2 o'clock and 3 o'clock is:

Come at two (o'clock).

    (*a*)   quarter past two.
        half past two.
    (*b*)   quarter to three.
        ten (minutes) to three.
        four minutes to three.

The word *minutes* is usually omitted for multiples of five but not for other numbers. *Quarter* is sometimes with article, *a quarter*.

2. A more formal way of expressing the time, used mainly for official functions, for programmes and timetables, and for transport (except planes), is to read the numbers as two groups, adding a.m. [ei em] and p.m. [pi: em] when it is necessary to show *morning* or *afternoon/evening* hours.

The train leaves at 10.00 p.m. (ten p.m.).

at 10.05 p.m. (ten five p.m.).

at 11.30 a.m. (eleven thirty a.m.).

3. For some purposes we use the international 24-hour system, especially for the times of international planes arriving at or leaving an airport, for military purposes and for official weather broadcasts and the checking of the course of ships or planes by radio.

The plane lands at 10.30 hours (ten thirty hours).

at 15.00 hours (fifteen hundred hours).

"Midnight" = 24.00 hours (twentyfour hundred hours).

The hours from midnight to 10 o'clock in the morning are written 01, 02, 03 etc.; the introductory nought is read as "o" [ou] or "zero" [ziərou].

The plane leaves at 03.30 hours (o-three thirty hours).

00.45 hours (o-o-fortyfive hours,

or zero-zero-fortyfive

hours).

Use only types 1 and 2 in this exercise.

Say the following times:

11.09; 9.30; 1.15; 3.45; 6.10; 7.25; 11.35; 12.45; 1.05; 2.50; 6.45; 6.40; 4.56; 12.00.

Section 9

" SOME " AND " ANY "

EXERCISE 17. Elementary

Note: The word "*some*" occurs first in Exercise 4. If we change such sentences into the negative, we must also change "*some*" into "*any*". This is also true for the compounds made with "*some*".

We have some books/bread.
We haven't any books/bread. (We don't have . . . U.S.)

I want something to eat.
I don't want anything to eat.

I saw somebody there.
I didn't see anybody there.

Most questions that can be answered with "yes" or "no" (that is, questions that do not begin with question-words: who? when? where? etc.) are made with "*any*" in place of "*some*".

We had some books/bread. Did you have any books/bread?

First make the following sentences negative, then interrogative:

1. I have some books.
2. He bought some ties.
3. There is some news.
4. They want some paper.
5. You ate some apples.
6. You asked some questions.
7. We shall have some rain.
8. The boy has some more cake.
9. I have seen you somewhere before.
10. He knows something.
11. They found it somewhere.
12. You have some.
13. You saw someone there.
14. He has sent me some letters.
15. He gave you some ink.
16. Put some more sugar in my tea.
17. There are some pictures in this book.
18. He told someone else.
19. I saw somebody at the window.
20. She wants some more like that.

EXERCISE 18. Elementary

Add "some" or "any" as required:

1. Please give me ... more pudding. I'm sorry but there isn't ...
2. Go and ask him for ... more paper. I haven't ... in my desk.
3. I have ... more letters for you to write.
4. I like those roses; please give me ... What a pity there aren't ... red ones.

5. I can't eat ... more potatoes, but I should like ... more beans.
6. I don't think there is ... one here who can speak French.
7. I must have ... ink and ... paper, or I can't write ... thing.
8. There aren't ... matches left; we must buy ... more.
9. Put ... salt on your meat, the cook hasn't put ...
10. You can have ... of my chocolate when you haven't ... more of your own left.
11. You can't have ... more dates because I want ... for myself.
12. There is ... tea in the kitchen, but there isn't ... milk.
13. I want to buy ... flowers; we haven't ... in the garden now.
14. He wants ... more pudding. Give him ...
15. Put ... bread on the table; we shall need ... more.

EXERCISE 19. Intermediate

Note: No. 4 of previous exercise has the plural form "ones". The words "one" and "ones" are used to replace countable nouns to avoid repetition after an adjective; they are not used after the possessive adjectives (*my, your etc.*).

Sentences expressing doubt, conditional sentences (with "if") and sentences with "scarcely", "hardly", "barely" etc. are counted as negatives and will have "any" instead of "some".

Add "some", "any" or "one(s)" as required:

1. I want ... new potatoes; have you ...?
2. You have a lot of apples; please give me ...
3. I asked him for ... soap, but he hadn't ...
4. These loaves are stale; please give me ... new ...
5. I want ... flour, but the grocer hasn't ...
6. I asked him for ... ink, and he gave me ...
7. So this is your house. It's a very pretty ...
8. I doubt if there are ... sweets left. You'd better give ... chocolate to the children that haven't had ...
9. I want ... oranges. Give me these big ...

10. You can take these eggs if you want ..., but I've ... better ... inside.
11. If you need ... more money, you must get ... out of the bank; there is hardly ... in the house.
12. They say the blue ... are best. I'll buy ... if you have ... left.
13. Don't make ... noise. He wants to get ... sleep.
14. Do you want ... bananas? Here are ... nice ripe ...
15. Are there ... more books? I've read all these old ...

EXERCISE 20. Elementary

Note: The forms with *"any"* and a negative verb in the last two exercises can sometimes be found as forms with *"no"* and an affirmative verb. The *"no"* forms are mainly used as short negative answers to question-word questions, the forms with *"not . . . any"* being more usual in ordinary negative statements. Ordinary statements with *"no"* forms are felt to be more emphatic.

We didn't go anywhere. We went nowhere (*emph.*).

You didn't give us any homework. You gave us no homework.

Change the following "no" forms into "not ... any" forms:

Students are reminded that several of the sentences below sound odd as they stand:

1. I have no time to help you.
2. There is no more sugar.
3. I can see my hat nowhere.

No. 3

hardly any

4. He wants no homework tonight.
5. We have seen nobody we know yet.
6. They want nothing to eat.
7. I have no more money.
8. There are no apples on the tree.
9. There was nobody in the garden.
10. The poor little boy has no shoes to wear.
11. There is nowhere for you to sleep.
12. The cook has put no salt in the cabbage.
13. They will do no more work.
14. There was nothing left.
15. The chicken has laid no eggs today.
16. I want no more, thank you.
17. He gave me nothing to drink.
18. I'll give it to nobody else.
19. He gave me no ink, so I could write no more.
20. My uncle can see nothing without his glasses.

EXERCISE 21. Elementary

Note: "Where are you going?" —"*Nowhere.*"
"What's the matter?"   —"*Nothing.*"

Do not forget that "neither" ("not . . . either") is used for two items, "none" ("not . . . any") for any larger number of countables or any quantity of an uncountable noun.

Answer the following in a short negative form:

1. Where are you going?
2. How many exercises have you done today?
3. Who were you talking to?
4. How much did these flowers cost?
5. What are you doing?
6. Where has she been?
7. Who did you meet?
8. Who phoned this morning?
9. How many will you give me?
10. What did you say?
11. Who told you to put it under the table?
12. What do they want?

13. Who do they want to see?
14. Which of these two books have you read?
15. How many have I given you already?
16. Who told you to do that?
17. What are you thinking about?
18. How many of these are mine?
19. Where did you go last night?
20. Which foot have you hurt?

Section 10

THE SPECIAL FINITES

Note: The above title includes all those verbs that are found *only* in the company of another verb; we can call these other verbs Full (or Ordinary) Verbs. The verbs **be, have** and **do** belong to both groups. This division is convenient for exercises on elementary sentence-structure because most of the patterns of everyday conversational English depend on the behaviour of these two classes of verb—Special Finites and Full Verbs. Here is a complete list of these Special Finites:

Be am is are was were	**May** might
Have has had	**Must** (have to, am to)
Do does did	**Ought** to
Shall should	**Used** to
Will would	**Need** (questions and negatives)
Can could	**·Dare** (questions and negatives)
Had better	**Would rather**

For short-form negative add *-n't*. Exceptions are *I'm not, can't, shan't, won't; had better not, would rather not*. These short forms should be used whenever the following exercises are done orally.

Distinguishing marks of the Special Finites are:

(a) No *-s* in 3rd person singular (except for **be, have** and **do**, which are also full verbs).

(b) Forms of **do** are not needed for making questions and negatives (except for certain uses of **have, need** and **used to**).

Full verbs regularly take *-s* in the 3rd person singular of the Present Simple Tense, and need the help of **do, does** or **did** to make questions or negatives.

EXERCISE 22. Elementary

Make the following sentences negative:

1. He must do it again.
2. She could understand everything.
3. They had time to tell her.
4. It was very late.
5. We're coming tomorrow morning.
6. He can speak French.
7. *He*'ll come if *you* can. (Falling stress on the two pronouns.)
8. You must come this morning.
9. He comes here every day.
10. We like her very much.
11. They arrived at six o'clock.
12. There were many people at the concert.
13. Why did you come with him?
14. We could see as far as the mountains.
15. You shall have another one tomorrow.
16. Our teacher wants the homework now.
17. You must look out of the window.
18. Eric can understand what you say.
19. There are some more cakes.
20. He has enough to eat.

EXERCISE 23. Elementary

Note: **Have,** if used with its fundamental meaning of "to own", or as an auxiliary verb for Perfect Tenses, does not need *do, does* or *did* for questions or negatives. (But notice that in American English the verb *do* is usual with **have** for almost all its meanings except the Perfect Tense forms.)

Answer the following questions in the negative:

1. Can you drink tea?
2. Mustn't you eat fish?
3. Ought you to have any coffee?
4. Can you stay up late?
5. Will you have another cigarette?
6. Couldn't he telephone?

7. Mustn't you go out so late at night?
8. Have you any other brothers or sisters?
9. Do you have lunch at one o'clock?
10. Can you speak Czech?
11. Did you read last night's paper?
12. Have you seen my hat anywhere?
13. Do stupid people always have stupid faces?
14. Ought he to work so hard?
15. Were there many people at the party?

EXERCISE 24.   Intermediate

Note: Compare the word-order of these two sentences:

(a) We *have painted* the house every year. (We, ourselves, paint it.)

(b) We *have* the house *painted* every year. (We pay someone to do it for us.)

Question and negative forms of (b) are always made with the help of *do, does* or *did.* The verb get can replace have.

  Examples: He must have (get) the pen mended.
      I had the car washed yesterday.

Change the following sentences by using "have" or "get" with a past participle:

1. Someone doesn't clean them for us every day.
2. I asked someone to paint the gate last week.
3. Someone tuned her piano for her yesterday.
4. Somebody will have to see to it for you.
5. I asked a man to mend my shoes.
6. Your hair wants cutting. You must ...

No. 6   BARBER'S
                                                          SHOP

7. Tell someone to translate it into English.
8. I'll ask someone to make a new one.
9. We ordered somebody to whitewash the ceiling.
10. The knives want sharpening. We must ...
11. We must find somebody to chop all this wood up.
12. Tell him to take another photograph.
13. I'm going to tell someone to add an extra room.
14. He asked his tailor to lengthen the trousers.

No. 14

15. Tell someone to bring it to you on a tray.

Notice also the similar construction **to have somebody do something,** more often used by American than British speakers:

She had someone paint the gate last week.
She had someone tune the piano yesterday.
You'll have to have someone see to it.

(*Do Nos.* 5, 7, 9, 11, 12, 14, 15, *in the same way.*)

EXERCISE 25. Elementary

Note: The verb MUST has no other forms; for other tenses and verb-forms we borrow from other expressions having a similar

B

meaning. The chief variant of **I must** for this purpose is **I have (got) to.**

> **He must go** and **He has (got) to go** tell us that it is *necessary* for him to go; an obligation.

> **He must not go (mustn't go)** and **He is not to go** tell us that it is *necessary* for him **not** to go; a prohibition.

These forms are both Present and Future. We can also express obligation in the Future by the form **He will have to go;** the present tense can replace this form if something else in the sentence tells us that it is future time:

> *We must begin at 8; we have (got) to begin at 8.*

Past obligation is usually expressed by **He had (got) to go.**

Past prohibition is usually expressed by **He was not to go;** this form is most commonly found in Indirect Speech:

> *He said we were not to be late.*

The forms using "got" (**I have got to go,** etc.) are more usual in spoken than in written English.

Summary:

	Obligation	Prohibition
Present	I must go I have (got) to go	I must not go I am not to go
Future	I must go I shall have to go	I must not go I am not to go
Past	I had (got) to go	I was not to go

I am (was etc.) **obliged to** can also express **must;** but notice that **I am not obliged to** is not the same as **I mustn't.** It means **I needn't.** (See Exercise 27.)

Make the following sentences negative; that is, change them into prohibitions:

1. You must leave this room.
2. He will have to stay longer.
3. They had to make a noise.
4. You'll have to read this book again.
5. They have to sell our house.
6. He must take it away.
7. He said you had to listen to them.
8. You must begin before 5 o'clock.
9. You'll have to wait for me tomorrow.
10. You must do it without help.

EXERCISE 26. Elementary

The following sentences are prohibitions; change them into obligations (that is, make them affirmative):

1. You mustn't stay here alone.
2. He is not to leave the house tomorrow.
3. He said we were not to read the whole book.
4. They're not to come again.
5. You mustn't eat this without salt.
6. He says I'm not to tell them your name.
7. They were not to open the classroom windows.
8. She mustn't go home alone.
9. He says you're not to write another letter.
10. The boys mustn't write in pencil.

EXERCISE 27. Elementary

Note: Look at these sentences:

"You **must** go now. No, you **needn't** go just yet, you can
(may) stay a little longer.

To express the absence of any obligation or necessity (that is,
the opposite of **must**), the form **need not** is used. Alternative forms
are borrowed from **to have to,** with its negative and question forms
made with *do.*

Summary of forms:

	Obligation	No obligation
Present	I must go I have (got) to go	I needn't go I don't have to go I haven't got to go
Future	I must go I shall have to go	(as above) or I shan't have to go I shan't need to go
Past	I had (got) to go	I hadn't got to go I didn't have to go I didn't need to go

I'm not obliged to go, etc., is another alternative for the right-hand column.

Read each of the following sentences as it stands, then in the negative form (that is, remove the idea of obligation or necessity):

1. I must get there before eight.
2. You will have to come again.
3. They must leave before dinner.
4. She must wash up all the glasses.
5. We had to change our shoes.
6. He had to give it back.
7. Our teacher must write it on the blackboard.
8. We had to finish it by today.
9. We shall have to leave earlier than usual.
10. You must answer at once.
11. We had to begin very early.
12. You'll have to bring your own ink with you.

13. You must eat them all.
14. I shall have to buy a new one.
15. They must learn the whole poem.
16. She has to make some new ones. (*N.B.* some–any)
17. I had to read it aloud.
18. She must wear a hat.
19. You'll have to stand outside.
20. You must do the whole exercise again.

EXERCISE 28. Elementary and Intermediate

Read each of the following sentences, then say (or write) it in the negative (that is, remove the idea of obligation):

1. He will have to pay me back before Christmas.
2. We had to bend it to get it into the box.
3. They must brush their own shoes.
4. They had to brush their own shoes every day.
5. You'll have to buy us some more.
6. She'll have to carry both of them.
7. We must change our clothes for dinner.
8. We had to cook them first.
9. She had to drink it without sugar.
10. We had to pay them for it, and we shall have to pay them some more next week.
11. You must put all the eggs in one basket.
12. Grandfather had to finish reading it in bed.
13. You must give it back to me before you go.
14. They had to light a fire to cook their supper.
15. You must listen to this talk on the radio.
16. We shall have to wait (*a*) long (time) for our holidays.
17. Last year we even had to book accommodation.
18. In any case we have to get train tickets, because we are taking our bicycles.
19. We shall have to take a lot of food with us.
20. We must even take a cooking stove.

EXERCISE 29.   Intermediate

Note: In Exercise 27 we met a past tense negative of *I needn't go*, namely **I didn't need to go.** Another past tense negative is **I needn't have gone,** but with an extended meaning.

I didn't need to go: I (probably) did not go, because it was not necessary.

I needn't have gone: I *did* go, although it was not necessary.

> *Examples:*   (a) My tea was already sweetened, so I didn't need to put any sugar in. (I drank it as it was.)
>
> (b) My tea was already sweetened, so I needn't have put any sugar in. (But I did, and so have made it too sweet.)

Put in the form "didn't need to" or "needn't have" according to the sense:

1. I ... (buy) a new one, so I've brought the old one back.
2. They ... (push) it into the corner, because it was there already.
3. She ... (fill) it so full, then it wouldn't have spilt.
4. We ... (open) the drawer, seeing that it was already open.
5. She ... (open) the drawer, seeing that she found it empty when she did.
6. I ... (pay) for it, because it was put on my father's account.
7. You ... (stay) if you hadn't wanted to.
8. I ... (take) my ink because I knew I should find some there.
9. I ... (tell) him personally, I wrote him a letter.
10. You ... (tell) me, but since you have, I'll do what I can for you.
11. You ... (wake) me up, there's another hour before the train leaves.
12. I ... (wake) him up, because he was already sitting on the bed, putting his socks on.
13. You ... (write) such a long composition, because I shan't have time to mark it.

14. I ... (ring) the bell, because the door opened before I got to it.

15. You ... (wait) for me, I could have found the way all right.

EXERCISE 30. Elementary and Intermediate

Note: **Can** has two main uses:
1. To express **ability** or **capacity** (=know how to).
2. To express **permission** (=may).

This second use is not recommended by some people, on the grounds that **may** is a special word that expresses just this idea. It has been quite common usage for so long, however, that it is now a natural part of English idiom. (A similar use of **can** is common to many other European languages.)

The other tenses of these two meanings are:

Future:	1. (ability)	**Shall (will) be able to.**
	2. (permission)	**Can.**
Past:	1. (ability)	**Was (were) able to;** or **could.**
	2. (permission)	**Could.**

Read the following sentences: (a) in the future tense; (b) in the past tense, using the given time expressions:

1. He can leave it here. (a) for an hour. (b) whenever he wanted to.

2. He can play chess: (a) this afternoon; (b) when he was young.

3. We can do this exercise: (a) next week; (b) last week.

4. She can cook very well: (a) with more practice; (b) when I knew her.

5. I can go early: (a) if he lets me; (b) every day last summer.

6. He says I can have another one: (a) tomorrow; (b) he said ... yesterday.

7. I can go swimming: (a) when it is warmer; (b) whenever I liked.

8. We can't find it: (a) until tomorrow; (b) when we looked for it.

9. John can stay up late: (a) tonight; (b) even when he was a small boy.

10. I can meet you: (*a*) on Saturday; (*b*) whenever I liked.
11. We can speak English: (*a*) soon; (*b*) when we were in London.
12. He can find a good answer: (*a*) if you ask him tonight; (*b*) whenever I asked him a question.
13. My father can help me: (*a*) when he comes home; (*b*) when he had time.
14. We can see the sea: (*a*) a little farther on; (*b*) from the top of the hill.
15. We can't understand: (*a*) until you explain it again; (*b*) when he spoke so quickly.

EXERCISE 31. Elementary

Note: Refer back to the list of Special Finites given before Exercise 22.

All these words make questions by inversion with the subject, and negatives by adding the word "not".

    Examples: He may come/may he come?/he may not come.
    It will rain/will it rain?/it will not (won't) rain.

Full verbs in the Present and Past Simple tenses use the Special Finite "do" in order to make questions or negatives.

    Examples: They go/do they go?/they don't go.
    He went/did he go?/he didn't go.

This basic principle is the key to rapid and idiomatic spoken English, because all the short responses of conversation follow exactly the same pattern. This can be expressed very briefly by the following two simple rules:

1. A Special Finite is echoed in the response.
2. A Full Verb appears as a form of "do" in the response. (The word "response" is used here to mean any kind of remark that is made as the result of some initial remark. It may be an answer to a question, an agreement, a contradiction; in fact any one of many possible "responses" to a person's remark. The next group of exercises will provide practice in most of the commoner conversational situations.)

Questions. There are two main types of question.

  (*a*) Those demanding *Yes/No* answers; they are made by inverting subject and verb.
  (*b*) Those demanding a new element in the answer; they begin with a question-word.

These next two exercises deal with the short answers to type (*a*):

      Are you a pupil?   *Yes, I am.*   *No, I'm not.*

      Do you study English? *Yes, I do.*   *No, I don't.*

Give short answers in the same way to the following questions:

1. Can you speak English?
2. Have you met my Uncle Jim?
3. Are you enjoying yourself?
4. Must I be there in time? Yes, ...
5. Did you meet him yesterday?
6. Does he play chess?
7. Could you come a little later?
8. Did you drink at all?
9. Oughtn't he to pay you at once? Yes, he ...
10. Does your sister like chocolates?
11. Did you say anything?
12. May I go out? Yes, you ...
13. Will your brother be there?
14. Were you at the cinema last night?
15. Are you reading?

EXERCISE 32. Elementary and Intermediate

Note: In Exercise 27 we saw that the opposite of **must** is **needn't.**
This is important to remember in responses to these two words.

      Examples: Need I get up so soon? *Yes, I'm afraid you must.*

                Must I finish it tonight? *No, you needn't.*

Used to. As this is one of the Special Finites on our list, it makes
questions and negatives as follows:

      You used to live here/Used you to live here?/You used not
      to live here. (You usedn't to . . .)

These forms are more often seen in print than heard in speech;
we frequently hear the following patterns in more informal
English. (They look a little strange but are accepted as good
spoken forms.) "I'm surprised to see John reading *The Times.*
Did he use [ju:s] to read *The Times?*"

"No, I'm sure he didn't use to read *The Times.*"

(or "No, he never used to read *The Times.*")

The word *never* is really a kind of emphatic negative in this last
sentence.

Ought to. When we say *You ought to do it*, we suggest either that it would be good for you to do it, (something desirable), or that we feel it is your duty to do it. Notice that in short answers we usually keep the infinitive particle with **ought to, used to** and **have to.**

Must I go now?

  (*a*) It's late; I think you ought to.

  (*b*) Yes, I'm afraid you have to.

Give short answers to the following questions:

1. Will it be fine this afternoon? *No, I'm afraid* ...
2. Would he come if I asked him? *No, I doubt whether* ...
3. Dare you climb this tall tree? *No, I* ...
4. Need we write our homework in ink? *Yes, I'm afraid* ...
5. Do you really think he used to live here?
        Response (*a*) *Yes, I* ...
        Response (*b*) *Yes, I'm sure he* ...
6. Did you have any difficulty with your homework?
7. Oughtn't you to read it once more? *Yes, we* ...
8. Do they all speak English as well as you? *Yes, they* ...
9. Must I really wait until you've finished? *Well, perhaps you* ... (neg.).
10. Does he want us to bring back some oranges? *Yes, he* ...
11. Oughtn't you to answer the letter at once? *Yes, I* ...
12. Need we take the exam? *Of course you* ...
13. Were you late for school? *No, I* ...
14. Shall we see you again soon? *Yes, I'm sure you* ...
15. Have you understood these sentences? *Yes, we* ...

EXERCISE 33. Elementary

Note: **Questions.** (See Exercise 31.) The second type of question is made with a question-word (*who? what? when?* etc.); the answer always has something new, and so can never be with yes/no. The same pattern of *Special Finite* or *do* may be used in the answer if this new element is the Subject.

       Who has done the homework? *We all have.*

       Who knows the next lesson? *John does.*

Give similar short answers to these questions:

1. Who wrote *Hamlet*?
2. Which of you must clean the blackboard?
3. How many of you play tennis?   Most of us ...
4. How many of you can play chess?   None of us ...
5. Who teaches you English?
6. What fell on the floor just now?
7. Which is better, this one or that one?
8. Which cost more, these or those?
9. How many of you ought to know the answer.   All of us ...
10. Who made that noise?
11. Which of you likes ice-cream?   We all ...
12. What fruit is good to eat?   All ...
13. How many of you must answer this question?   We all ...
14. Who shut the door?
15. Which gives more light, the sun or the moon?
16. What makes people fat?   Eating ...
17. Who discovered America?
18. What was the world's biggest island before Australia was discovered?
19. Which weighs more, a pound of feathers or a pound of lead?
20. What's the capital of Iceland?
21. How many of you have breakfast before seven in the morning?
22. Who likes chocolate?
23. Who came late today?
24. Who taught you to swim?
25. How many of you ought to do more homework?   We all ...

EXERCISE 34.   Elementary

Note: **Agreement.** A similar pattern is used for agreeing with a remark that someone has made. The three most usual words for introducing an agreement are:

(a) **Yes,** for simple factual agreement.
    Example: It's hot today.   *Yes, it is.*
                It looks like rain.   *Yes, it does.*

(b) **So,** for showing surprise.
    Example: There's some flour on your shoe. *So there is.*
                You've dropped some papers.   *So I have.*

(c) **Of course,** for something that is clearly true.
    Example: I expect we shall win the competition. *Of course*
                   we shall.
                My sister likes chocolate. *Of course she does.*

Agree with the following remarks, read to you by your teacher:

1. Ahmed is late again.   *Yes ...*
2. The clock has lost a hand!   *So ...*
3. That music sounds pleasant.   *Yes ...*
4. You've got some ink on your sleeve.   *So ...*
5. I'm sure you will all learn English quickly.   *Of course ...*
6. Your book has fallen on the floor.   *So ...*
7. We must water the garden this evening.   *Yes ...*
8. Perhaps your teacher is right.   *Of course ...*
9. She ought to go home soon.   *Yes ...*
10. They must pay us back the money.   *Of course ...*
11. He swims better than his friend.   *Yes ...*
12. You've spilt some coffee on your sleeve!   *So ...*
13. You must do as your father tells you.   *Of course ...*
14. There's a hole in your coat!   *So ...*
15. I can speak English quite well.   *Of course ...*

EXERCISE 35.   Elementary and Intermediate

Note: **Disagreement.** When we disagree with a remark that someone has made, we respond with "No" or "Oh no" and follow with the same kind of verb patterns as before.
    Examples: This box is too heavy for you. *(Oh) no, it isn't.*
                They want to tell you something. *(Oh) no, they*
                   don't.
Sometimes we begin with "Oh, but ...". This is for disagreeing with a question (usually with "why?").
    Example: Why did you tell her? *(Oh), but I didn't.*

Do not forget Exercise 27 on **must** and **needn't**.

> *Example:* I suppose I must be home before 5. *Oh no, you needn't.*

Disagree with the following remarks, read to you by your teacher:

1. You've done this exercise before.
2. Don't hurry, we have plenty of time.
3. Why are you so angry?
4. He has plenty of money.
5. I feel sure this dog will bite me. *Oh no, it ...*
6. Your friend can lend you the money.
7. You've made a mistake.
8. How did you break your pen?
9. The door's locked.
10. You ought to do at least five homeworks a week.
11. I arrived long before you.
12. I was here long before you.
13. The other boys can come tomorrow.
14. I wrote it on the blackboard last week.
15. Why did you write the exercise in pencil?
16. I suppose we must wait for the others.
17. You've lost your new handkerchief.
18. You'll be late if you don't hurry.
19. Why must I wait till the end?
20. You can easily beat him at chess.

EXERCISE 36.   Elementary and Intermediate

Note: **Disagreement with a Negative.** If the remark that we disagree with is a negative, we respond with "(Oh), yes . . ." and the appropriate Special Finite.

> You *can't* eat all that!   (Oh), yes, I *can*.
> You *didn't* hear me.   (Oh), yes, I *did*.

A negative question (this is most often with "Why?") has a disagreement response beginning with "Oh, but . . ."

Why didn't you write to me? *Oh, but I did.*

Pupils should notice these two important points on how to speak the two disagreement responses of Exercises 35 and 36.

1. The commas after *Oh* and *Yes/No* are usual in writing, **but** we do not make a pause when speaking.
2. The two forms (**Yes/No** and **But**) have different intonation patterns:

    Yes/No has a fall *either* on the **Oh** *or* on **Yes/No,** followed by a rise (or fall-rise) on the verb.

    But is quite low and unstressed until we reach the verb, which falls rapidly from a high tone.

    (Further explanations and exercises on these points can be found in "Living English Speech", by the same author and publisher.)

    Do not forget Exercise 27 on **must** and **needn't.**

    The disagreement with **needn't** usually begins with (*Oh*), *but* . . . .

    You needn't give it back. (*Oh*), *but I must.*

    You needn't have paid me back. (*Oh*), *but I had to.*

Disagree with the following remarks, read to you by your teacher:

1. You can't read this!
2. I haven't any paper! (*Amer.* I don't have any paper!)
3. We don't have coffee for breakfast.
4. He won't understand us!
5. I know you don't like chocolate!
6. You couldn't understand a single word!
7. Why can't you write more neatly! (*but*)
8. It wasn't me you saw!
9. I'm not late today!
10. You can't see the blackboard from there!
11. You didn't pay him for the book.
12. Why didn't you tell me his name? (*but*)
13. I'm not stupid, you know!
14. Well, *you're* not very clever!
15. She needn't come tomorrow. (*but*)
16. Your mother won't like this film.
17. You needn't pay for it! (*but*)
18. I'm not going to enjoy this book.
19. Why won't he believe you? (*but*)
20. You needn't have given it back to him. (*but*) (*and see Ex.* 29).

EXERCISE 37.   Elementary

Note: **Additions to remarks made.**

An **affirmative** addition is made by introducing the suitable Special Finite with "so", and putting the new subject *after* the verb.

> *Examples:* John likes homework. *So do I.*
> He must go. *So must the others.*

Do not confuse this use of **so** with the one without inversion in Exercise 34.   Compare the following:

You've dropped your book. So I have! *(surprised agreement)*
You've dropped your book. So has he. *(addition)*

We use the same pattern for adding either to someone else's remark or to our own.

Read the following remarks and add to them, using the suggestions between brackets:

1. He came early. (I)
2. You can come whenever you like. (your friend)
3. Apples were very dear. (bananas)
4. He ought to listen more carefully. (you)
5. My friend lives in Chicago. (his sister)
6. A stone sinks. (iron)
7. Watt was an inventor. (Edison)
8. Mary could do it. (her teacher)
9. Dogs like meat. (cats)
10. They must do as they are told. (you)
11. Browning wrote poetry. (Tennyson)
12. She must go home. (I)
13. Dick wrote me a letter. (his mother)
14. I like sweets. (we all)
15. The potatoes are too salty. (beans)

EXERCISE 38.   Elementary

Note: **Additions to remarks made.**

A **negative** addition is made in the same way as in the previous exercise, introducing the response with **nor** or **neither;** there will be inversion of the new subject.

Examples: He can't read this. *Nor (neither) can I.*
Potatoes won't grow here. *Nor (neither) will roses.*

Read the following remarks and add to them, using the suggestions between brackets:

1. Dogs don't fly. (pigs)
2. Dogs can't fly. (cats)
3. He wasn't late. (you)
4. He hasn't any time. (I)
5. These books don't belong to me. (those)
6. These aren't my books. (those)
7. He oughtn't to make such a mistake. (you)
8. We couldn't remember his name. (they)
9. Water hasn't any taste. (this soup)

No. 9

10. John didn't stay to supper. (Henry)
11. I don't believe it. (my friend)
12. I have never been to Berlin. (he)
13. This clock doesn't show the right time. (my watch)
14. Animals don't like the hot weather. (I)
15. Joan can't eat fish. (my cousin Tom)

EXERCISE 39. Elementary

Note: **Contrary Additions.**
The Special Finite of this response is introduced by **but;** ordinary word-order. The stress falls on the new subject, with a rising intonation on the verb.

Examples: He can read French . . . but *she* **can't.**
We arrived early   . . . but *you* didn't.
We **must** leave early . . . but *you* **needn't.**

(As in Exercises 37 and 38, the response may be made either by the speaker or a second person.)

Read the following remarks and add the new subject in the contrary sense:

1. We can come tomorrow. (*they*)
2. I have a lot of time. (*he*)
3. My knife cuts very well. (*my friend's*)
4. Her dress looked lovely. (*she*)
5. You were very late. (*your teacher*)
6. The others went for a swim. (*I*)
7. Tom spoke to us. (*Henry*)
8. I know the town very well. (*he*)
9. I can write with my left hand. (*you*)
10. I must get there very early. (*you*)
11. He's a very good student. (*you*)
12. The buses were full. (*the trams*)
13. He always makes mistakes. (*I*)
14. You had to wait. (*I*)
15. I left early. (*my brother*)

EXERCISE 40.   Elementary

Note: **Contrary Additions.**

As for previous exercise; this exercise adds responses to negative remarks.

Example: He can't read French . . . but *she* can.

Read the following remarks and add the new subject in the contrary sense:

1. He doesn't understand you. (*I*)
2. The man won't know the answer. (*the woman*)
3. Grapes aren't cheap now. (*figs*)
4. I don't like cowboy films. (*my brother*)
5. He didn't listen to the lecture. (*I*)

6. You needn't get there very early. *(the others)*
7. A cat can't swim very well. *(a dog)*
8. She doesn't want to come. *(her sister)*
9. My friend couldn't explain. *(I)*
10. We haven't seen the new pupil. *(Henry)*
11. He won't tell you the answer. *(his friend)*
12. The teacher needn't write in ink. *(the pupils)*
13. He won't leave tomorrow. *(we)*
14. They couldn't hear what the lecturer said. *(we)*
15. The boys didn't need to wait long. *(the girls)*

EXERCISE 41. Elementary

Note: **Question-tags.**

This subject is practised more fully in Exercises 85 and 86. A "tag" is something small tied loosely to a larger object (for example, the label tied on the handle of a suitcase). It is used here to describe the little question phrase we attach to a statement to change it into a kind of rhetorical question. Most languages have one fixed phrase for this (for example, n'est-ce pas? nicht wahr? değil-mi? أليس كذلك).

In English we add an appropriate echo of the verb we have just used, repeating the Special Finite or using *do, does,* or *did.* An affirmative sentence has a negative tag; a negative sentence has an affirmative one.

> *Examples:* You *are* coming soon, *aren't* you?
> He *hasn't* seen it, *has* he?
> You *know* her, *don't* you?
> You *didn't* see her, *did* you?

Read each of the following and add a question-tag:

1. He is French.
2. We are late.
3. They weren't angry.
4. They have two children.
5. You understand it.
6. You'll tell us.
7. He isn't our teacher.
8. I mustn't be late.
9. He can explain.
10. We shall see you to-morrow.
11. You've torn your dress.
12. You came by tram.
13. I wasn't long.
14. She has just come.
15. They couldn't do it.
16. Dinner's ready.
17. You've taken it.

18. You needn't go yet.   20. They must come again.
19. He can have another one.

EXERCISE 42. Elementary

Note: **Agreement with a Negative.**

In Exercise 34 we practised responses for agreeing with an Affirmative. To agree with a Negative remark we normally use a short-form response followed by a question-tag. Both parts are always spoken with falling intonation.

    Examples:

"He *wasn't* late last time."   "No, *he wasn't, was he.*"
"He *scarcely ate* anything."   "No, *he didn't, did he.*"
"We *mustn't* be late."   "No, *we mustn't, must we.*"

A question mark could perhaps be added, but the sense does not really demand one. The word "no" is normally unstressed in this response, being joined to the following words as if there were no comma separating them.

Using the above question-tag pattern, agree with the following negative remarks:

1. They won't like it.
2. We can't cross the street here.
3. You didn't come early enough.
4. We aren't clever enough.
5. He wasn't at the party. *was he*
6. It hasn't rained for weeks.
7. We haven't come very far.
8. There isn't enough for us all.

No. 8

9. It's not a very big house.
10. You mustn't put your feet on the chair.
11. They didn't give us very good cakes.
12. Your shoes aren't very clean.
13. She can't sing so well as her sister.
14. This chair wasn't broken yesterday.
15. I'm not very good at English.

EXERCISE 43. Elementary

Note: A similar response is used for agreeing with an Affirmative remark, instead of the kinds practised in Exercise 34.

> *Examples:* "You're rather late." "Yes, *I am, aren't I.*"
> "He *came* too late." "Yes, *he did, didn't he.*"
> (Double falling stress as in Ex. 42.)

Using the above question-tag pattern, agree with the following affirmative remarks:

1. I'm rather sleepy today.
2. We shall have to go at once.
3. We've come a long way.
4. It rained hard last night.
5. There'll be enough for him, too.
6. It's a very large school.
7. They swam very well.
8. You must leave earlier today.
9. They gave us a lovely tea.
10. This chair has been mended.
11. I'm very good at English.
12. You're getting fat.
13. It was very hot yesterday.
14. The apples will soon be ripe.
15. You'll have to do it all again.

Section II

THE VERB

EXERCISE 44. Elementary

Note: **Imperative.** This form is used for making requests and giving orders; it is the same as the root-form that we find in the dictionary.

In this exercise the students are to make the imperatives as requested. It is best to take only parts of this exercise scattered over many class periods, and not to work solidly through it as one piece. It can be combined with similar practice in the Present Continuous tense (see Exercise 45).

Get the pupils to use "Please" when making requests.

BOOKS SHUT. (The pupils are to do what they **are asked**.)

Tell X to:

open (shut) his/her book, box, mouth, eyes, bag, desk, etc. . . .

stand in the corner, by me, on a chair, near the window, on one foot.

take . . . off the desk, a book from me.

push the door, X, a book off the desk, me into the corner.

hold a book, X's hand, up his hand, his nose.

make a mark on the board, a noise like a pig, cat, cow, dog, etc.

tell (you) the time, the date, his name, the teacher's name.

meet you after school, at the corner of the street, at 5 o'clock.

tear some paper, his/her handkerchief.

hide his pencil, face, rubber (eraser), etc.

. . . and any other requests with verbs known to the class.

The Negative Imperative is made with **Don't** followed by the infinitive.

Don't make so much noise!

Don't eat in class!

A few negative imperatives can be practised in the same way if suitable examples occur naturally in the lesson. Here are a few that *might* be possible:

Tell X **not** *to*:

Talk to his neighbour, **whisper, talk** so loudly.
Play with his pen, pencil, books, tie.
Push his neighbour, **kick** his neighbour (friend).
Bite his pencil, nails, lips.
Copy from his friend's book.
Look at the ceiling, out of the window.
Go to sleep, **fall** asleep, **yawn.**
Lay his hands on the desk.
Lend something to, **borrow** something from Y.
Forget his homework.
Listen to what Z says.
Think so hard, **look** so unhappy.

EXERCISE 45.   Elementary

Note: **Present Tense** (**Continuous**). Made from the present of "to be" with the "-ing" form of the verb. *He is going, we are coming, etc.* This is the tense we use to describe the actual present moment, NOW. This makes it especially useful for practical exercises in class. Some of the examples in Exercise 44 can be used here to practise the tense in the following pattern of questions and answers.

X, please shut the window. What is X doing? (*He is shutting . . .*)
What are you doing, X? (*I am shutting . . .*)

(Do not introduce new verbs into this exercise without learning them first.)
BOOKS SHUT.

    Stand up (on your desk), X. What is he (are you) doing?
                   Do the same with:
    Walk to the door (window, back of the room, **round the** room/table, etc.);
    take Y out of the room (to the door, round the room, by the hand, etc.);
    eat a sweet (sandwich, nut); **leave** the room; **stand** on a chair

(by the door, near the clock, beside me, etc.); **read** from your book (the next sentence, your homework, from the board, etc.); **write** on the board (your name, a sentence, numbers, etc.); **count** the students (the windows, these books/papers, your fingers, the desks, etc.); **fetch (bring) me** a piece of chalk (a piece of paper, a pencil, **the duster,** the wastepaper basket, Y's homework, your hat/pen/pencil, etc.); take a book out of the cupboard (a pencil from Y's desk, the duster to Y); **tear/cut/fold** some paper (this newspaper, your handkerchief, etc.).

Use any other verbs learnt.

N.B.—It is not advisable to try this exercise with verbs that are of very short duration, such as **throw, drop,** or **break,** because the action will end before you can ask questions in the Present Continuous form, and thus make the situation unreal!

EXERCISE 46.   Elementary

Note: **Present Tense (Simple).** This tense is the same as the infinitive (root form) of the verb. Unlike the **Continuous** form, the **Simple** present tense does not really describe *present* action. It is used for permanent or general statements, and to describe acts that are habitual or usual.

> *Examples:* The sun **shines** by day (habitually); it **is shining** now.   (real present)
>
> I **speak** English quite well (usually); I **am speaking** English now.   (real present)

Notice that **when?** cannot be used with the Present Continuous tense, except in the special use of this tense to express the immediate or certain Future.

BOOKS SHUT.

When (where) do we ...

go to sleep; **wake up**; **eat**; **drink**; **open (shut)** our books; **do** our homework; **have** lunch (breakfast, supper); **cry**; **laugh**; **learn** English; **eat** ice-cream; **make** a special cake; **play** games; **see** snow; **say** "Hello"; **sit down**; **put** our clothes on; **take** our clothes off; **wash** our hands; **sing**; **switch (put) on** the light; **go** to the cinema; **have** examinations; **listen** to our teacher, etc., etc.

EXERCISE 47.   **Elementary and Intermediate**

Note: **Present Tense** (**Simple**). The third person singular ends in "s". This exercise practises the ending, which students some-times carelessly omit.

Note the 3 pronunciations of this ending:

1. [iz] after s, z; ∫; t∫, dʒ.
     He passes, washes, watches, judges.
2. [s] after all voiceless consonants not included above.
     He cuts, takes, stops, laughs.
3. [z] after all voiced consonants not included under 1 above, and all vowel-sounds.
     He comes, rides, sings, goes, says.

Read these sentences in the singular:

1. They **sit** at the window and **watch** the traffic.
2. They **wash** their hands and **dry** them on a towel.
3. They **hit** their dog with a stick when they **are** angry with it.
4. Birds **build** their nests in the summer and **fly** to the south in the winter.
5. The children **play** all the morning and **sleep** in the afternoon.
6. My friends **like** meat, but **do** not like fish.
7. They **live** in small houses which **have** only three rooms.
8. His brothers **work** hard all day, and **want** to rest in the evening.
9. They **have** breakfast at eight o'clock and **eat** their lunch at half-past one.
10. They **want** to buy some toys, because their sons have a birthday tomorrow.
11. These boys **say** that they always **listen** carefully, but **do** not always understand their teachers because they **speak** too quickly and **choose** very difficult words.
12. Careful students always **put** back the books they **have** read before they **take** out others. These girls **come** to our library every Thursday and **read** a book every week; they **like** English and **want** to learn quickly.
13. Our friends **leave** for Alexandria at three today and

arrive there about seven; they **spend** their holidays there every year and **swim** in the sea or **sleep** nearly all the time. They **forget** their work, **enjoy** the sea air and **live** as free as birds. Their holidays **finish** in August, they **catch** an early train back to Cairo and **feel** well and happy when they **return** to work.

14. The boys **wake** up at seven o'clock, **wash, dress** quickly and **run** into the dining-room for breakfast. They **wait** until they **hear** the bell and then **go** to school.

15. My friends **tell** me that professors **are** people who **think** a lot, but **say** little, and that school-teachers **are** people who **say** a lot but **think** little.

EXERCISE 48. Elementary

Note: **Present Tenses.** Look once again at the difference between the Simple and Continuous forms (see examples in note to Exercise 46).

Present Simple. Habitual actions and general **truths; not** necessarily NOW.

Present Continuous. An action in progress NOW (at **this** moment).

(This tense is sometimes called **Present Progressive.**)

Put in the correct Present Tense of the given verbs:

1. She (go) to school every day.
2. We now (learn) English.
3. The sun always (shine) in Egypt.
4. I (sit) on a chair and (eat) a banana.
5. Bad students never (work) hard.
6. It (rain) in winter. It (rain) now.
7. I (wake up) at seven and (have) breakfast at half past.
8. He generally (sing) in English but today he (sing) in French.
9. The teacher (point) at the blackboard when he (want) to explain something.
10. Mother (cook) some food in the kitchen at present; she always (cook) in the mornings.

11. I always (meet) you on the corner of this street.
12. The baby (cry) because it is hungry now.
13. I (spend) this week-end in Alexandria. I (go) there nearly every week.
14. "Where are you?" "I (sit) in the kitchen." "What you (do) there?" "I (help) my mother."
15. "Where you (go) now?" "I (go) to the theatre." "I (go) tonight also, but I (not go) very often." "I (go) every week, but tonight I (go) for the second time in three days."

EXERCISE 49.   Intermediate

Note: **Present Tenses.** There are a few verbs that are seldom found in a **Continuous** form, unless used in some special sense. It is not possible to find a name that fairly describes all these verbs, but they are mostly verbs of sense, feeling or perception. These verbs describe actions or states that are not strictly under our control; they happen automatically. Look at the following:

     I **see** a man outside; he **is looking** at me.

Both verbs are about NOW, the Real Present; but "see" is not normally found in a continuous form. We have no control over what we see; we **see** whenever our eyes are open, but we can decide what to **look at,** and can change the direction of our eyes from one NOW to the next. Similarly with verbs like "understand"; we either "understand" or we "don't understand", we cannot "be understanding" for one moment, and the next moment "not be understanding". (A list of the commonest verbs of this type is added to the end of this exercise.)

Another important use of the Present Continuous is to announce a Future event which is already *fixed* or *arranged*. It is especially common with verbs of movement, but is not found with any of the verbs in the list at the end of this exercise. We could call it the **Arranged Future** (see also Exercise 66).

     Examples: I'm flying to New York tomorrow.
                 (I already have the tickets.)
            My uncle is coming to dinner on Friday.
                 (He has accepted our invitation.)
            We are having some new reading books next week.
                 (Our teacher has told us so.)

Put the verbs into the correct Present Tense form:

1. Ships (travel) from Southampton to New York in four or five days.

2. John (travel) to England tomorrow.

3. On my way to work I generally (meet) many children who (go) to school.

4. Look, a man (run) after the tram. He (want) to catch it.

5. It (be) very cold now. ?You (think) it (freeze)?

6. The sun (warm) the air and (give) us light.

7. "What you (read) when you are on holiday?" "I (read) detective stories. Now I (read) *The Shut Door* by Ivor Lock."

8. "?You (hear) anything?" "I (listen) hard but I can't hear anything."

9. "I (see) that you (wear) your best clothes. ?You (go) to a party?" "No, I (go) to a wedding." "And who is the unhappy man who (throw) away his freedom? You must tell him I (feel) sorry for him." "He (speak) to you now!"

No. 9

10. "?You (speak) French?" "I only (use) a foreign language when I (travel) abroad."

11. My friends (work) very hard. John (study) for an examination now.

12. Joan (swim) very well, but she (not dive).

13. "What music you (play) next?" "Sheila (sing) a song by Schubert; she (sing) it very well."

14. Wood (float) on water, but iron (not float).

15. "?You (understand) the present tense now?"
    "I (do) an exercise on it at this moment and I (think) that I (know) how to use it now."

Here is a list of common verbs that are not usually found in continuous forms:

> have (in the sense of Exercise 23 only), be (except in Passive voice);
>
> see, hear, smell, taste, notice, recognize;
>
> remember, recollect, forget, know, understand;
>
> believe, feel (that), think (that);
>
> suppose, mean, gather (that);
>
> want, wish, desire, refuse, forgive;
>
> care, love, hate, (dis)like;
>
> seem, appear (=seem), contain (=hold), consist of, possess, matter, own.

EXERCISE 50. Elementary

Note: **Present Perfect Tense.** This very common tense is one that a foreign learner usually finds difficult to use properly. He frequently confuses it with the past tense, occasionally with the present tense.

All three perfect tenses (past, present and future) tell us that some act is completed (=perfected) by a given time; for an act done *at a certain time* we use a *simple* tense.

Examples: (a) I wrote the letter yesterday.
(b) I had written the letter before he came.

(a) I write letters every week-end.
(b) I have already written two letters.

(a) I shall write the letter on Monday.
(b) I shall have written the letter by Monday.

The (b) sentences *do not state the time* of the action; the (a) sentences *give dates*.

So the **Present Perfect** . . .

1. Tells us about an act completed (=perfected) by **now**.
2. Is a kind of **Present** tense because
    (a) it does *not* tell us **when** this completed act happened;
    (b) we are interested only in its present completed state and its relation to **now**.

I have already written two letters: Here and now are two finished letters.

> "**I haven't written any letters yet:** Up to this present moment there are no letters finished."

We see that we cannot use the Present Perfect tense if a definite time in the past is either mentioned or understood from the context. For the same reason a question with **When?** cannot be in this tense. (The following oral drill introduces the tense from the imperative and/or present continuous tense. Further ideas can be freely arranged from Exercises 44 and 45.)

BOOKS SHUT. (*Substitute your pupils' names.*)

1. John, open your book at page 25. (What is he doing?).
   What have you (just) done, John?

2. Mary, go slowly to the door, (please). Where are you going, Mary?
   (To Henry.) Where has Mary gone?

3. Peter, say to Mary, "Go back to your place."
   (Or: ... tell Mary to go ...)
   What has Peter just said?
   Where are you going, Mary?
   Now where has Mary gone, Ann?

4. William, shut the window, please. (What is he doing?)
   What have you done, William?

5. (*Teacher drops chalk.*) What have I done (dropped), George?

6. (*Teacher slowly picks up chalk.*) What am I picking up, Freda?
   What have I put on my desk, Vera?

7. Jane, please write your name on the board.
   What is she doing, Shirley?
   What have you done, Jane?

8. Arthur, walk slowly to the window, please.
   What is he doing, Alfred?
   What have you done, Arthur?

9. Tom, say to Arthur, "Stay at the window."
   (... tell Arthur to stay ...)
   What has he just said to (told) Arthur?

10. *Teacher throws chalk at an inattentive pupil and asks.*
    someone else what he has just done.

11. John, read the first three sentences on page 20.
    (Mary, what is he (doing) reading?)
    What have you just done, John?

12. Paul, please give your exercise book (notebook) to George.
Paul, what have you just given to George?
George, what has Paul written on page 1?

13. Have you done (written) any homework for me today, John?

14. (**To someone at the back**.) Jim, go to the blackboard, please.
(Where is he going, Henry?)
Now please rub out Jane's name.   (see 7)
What is he doing, Tom?
What have you (done) rubbed out, Jim?

15. What are you doing at the window, Arthur? (see 9)
(How long has he been at the window, George?)

16. Freda, say to Arthur, "Walk slowly (back) to your place."
(Or: ... tell Arthur to walk ...)
What are you doing, Arthur?
John, what has Arthur just done?

17. Have you seen ... (name of current film)?
Who (else) has seen this film?

18. Have you (ever) read a Shakespeare play, Alfred?
(*Or an English story, a poem, etc.*) What story etc. have you read?

19. Have you ever eaten an English breakfast? fish soup? apple pie?   toast?   mangoes?   Christmas   pudding? raspberries?

20. Mary, have we read anything today?
Has (*name of pupil in No.* 10) given the chalk back to me (yet)?
(What have you done with my chalk, X?)
Where is the chalk now, John?
Have you learnt anything in this lesson?
What have you learnt?

EXERCISE 51.   Elementary

Note: **Present Perfect Tense.** Apart from the two adverbs expressing the idea by **now**, (the affirmative **already** and the negative **not yet**), which because of their meaning are normally found with the Present Perfect tense, the words **since** and **for** are also commonly used with this tense.

Since is *always* associated with the Perfect Tense. **For** is also used with this tense when it means "a length of time up to NOW". Note carefully the meanings of these two words.

Since means "from some definite *point* or *period* in the past till NOW".

(*Since yesterday, 2 o'clock, last year, 1950, we met you,* etc.)

For means "a *length* of time till NOW".

(*For a day, 2 hours, some months, a long time,* etc.)

Examples: I haven't seen you since Monday (since 1950).
I haven't seen you for a week (for five years).

Last. Be careful of this word. Look at these sentences:

I haven't seen you since last month.

I haven't seen you for *the* last month.

Last month (no article) refers to the last calendar month, and is therefore a period of time in the past from which we are measuring up to now. (= since April, May etc.)

The last month (with definite article) means the *length* of one month (i.e. about 30 days) up to now.

So *without* the definite article we use **since**; *with* it we use **for**.

Complete the following sentences with each of the given alternative endings by inserting **since** *or* **for**:

1. I haven't seen you ...
   (*a*) Christmas; (*b*) three days.
2. We've been here ...
   (*a*) an hour and a half; (*b*) January.
3. She hasn't spoken to me ...
   (*a*) more than two years; (*b*) last week.
4. They have lived in this street ...
   (*a*) 1919; (*b*) the last ten years; (*c*) a long time.
5. I haven't had time to do it ...
   (*a*) I was ill; (*b*) last Monday.
6. We haven't bought any new ones ...
   (*a*) a week; (*b*) ages; (*c*) then.
7. There hasn't been a famine ...
   (*a*) centuries; (*b*) the Middle Ages.

8. I haven't eaten any meat ...
   (a) over a year; (b) I was a little boy (girl).
9. Nobody has written to me ...
   (a) many weeks; (b) my birthday.
10. You've asked the same question every day ...
    (a) the beginning of the year; (b) the last fortnight.
11. You haven't sent me any money ...
    (a) last Saturday; (b) fifteen days.
12. She has worn the same old dress ...
    (a) at least a month; (b) the beginning of the month.
13. I haven't spoken Spanish ...
    (a) 1950; (b) ten years.

No. 14

14. I haven't ridden a bicycle ...
    (a) longer than I can remember; (b) my childhood.
15. It hasn't rained here ...
    (a) more than a month; (b) March.

EXERCISE 52. Intermediate

Note: **Present Perfect Continuous Tense.**

Sometimes we wish to describe an action that is not *completed* by the present moment, but is still going on. We want to join to the idea of the Present Perfect a further idea of the Present Continuous. This needs the continuous form of the Present Perfect, which we make quite regularly with the Present Perfect of the verb "to be" followed by the Present Participle ("-ing" form) of our main verb.

I have been/standing; he has been/sitting, etc.

THE VERB

This tense is especially common with "static" verbs (actions that do not finish quickly), such as:

sit, stand, wait, lie, learn, study, live, sleep, rest, etc.

(In fact such verbs are more often found in a continuous form than otherwise.)

> *Examples:* He is lying on the floor. (now)
> He has been lying there for three hours.
>   (=and there he is now, still lying)
> I'm writing a letter to my friend. (now)
> I've written two letters already.
>   (=here they are, complete)
> I've been writing letters all the morning
>   (*Amer.* "all morning"). (=and I'm still in
>   the middle of writing letters)

Read the following sentences, putting the verbs into the correct form of the Present Perfect (Simple or Continuous). The first ten sentences are all in the Continuous form:

1. I (live) here since 1950.
2. He (work) in this factory for ten years.
3. ?"You (wait) long for me?"
   "Yes. I (stand) here in the rain for half an hour."
4. Look! That light (burn) all night.
5. Lunch is not quite ready yet, although I (cook) all the morning. (*Amer.* all morning.)
6. He (learn) English for three years, but he can't even read a newspaper yet.
7. The cat (sit) in front of the fire all day.
8. "I (look) at this picture for the last five minutes, but I can't see you in it."
   "I'm afraid you (look) at the wrong one."
9. You must wake her up. She (sleep) soundly for more than ten hours.
10. How long (you learn) English?
11. I (look for) my pen all day, but I (not find) it yet.
12. That book (lie) on the table for weeks. ?You (not read) it yet?
13. I (not see) you for a long time.

C

14. I (try) to learn English for years, but I (not succeed) yet.
15. You already (drink) three cups of tea since I (sit) here.
16. I (wait) here for my friend since five o'clock, but he (not come) yet.
17. My watch (go) for three days and it (not stop) yet.
18. That fine tree (stand) near our home ever since I was a boy. I'm glad they (not cut) it down yet.
19. They (shut up) the house and (go away) for a holiday.
20. I know you (talk) about grammar for the last half an hour, but I'm afraid I (not listen)!

This tense is also used when the action is not in fact still going on; this is when the speaker wishes to inform us that the action was continuous, though it is not still continuing. It is Present Perfect because it is the result of such continuous activity that now holds the speaker's interest.

Examples: I'm cold because I've been swimming for over an hour.
I must sit down for five minutes; I've been running round the town all day. (The speaker does not mean this literally; he (or she) has been walking about the town all the time, shopping perhaps.) The last example in the note to this exercise might also carry this meaning, *i.e.* that I'm not writing at the moment, but I've been hard at it most of the time; there is still some more time left this morning for me to go on with my letter-writing.

EXERCISE 53. Intermediate

Note: **Revision of Present Perfect** (Simple and Continuous), and **since** and **for**.

Put the verb in the correct form of the Present Perfect tense, and add "since" or "for":

1. I (wait) here ... five o'clock.
2. I (write) letters ... the last two hours.
3. She (not wear) that dress ... two years.
4. I (read) two novels ... yesterday.
5. We (study) English ... only six months.

6. "How long that fire (burn)?"
   " ... last night."
7. Coal (get) dearer ... last year.
8. ?"You (see) John lately?"
   "Not ... three or four days."
9. I (write) four letters ... breakfast.
10. I'm sure that boy (not wash) his face ... yesterday.
11. ?"You (visit) your uncle recently?"
    "Not ... last Monday."
12. I (stand) here ... half an hour, but the bus (not come) yet.
13. How many words you (learn) ... our last lesson?
14. We (sit) on these hard seats ... nearly an hour.
15. "How often you (speak) to him recently?"
    "Twice ... last week."

Notice that the Present Perfect is often used with **this** *week, month, year, morning*, etc., because the period of time is still with us, which brings the action up to the speaker's NOW. An interesting but quite logical exception is with the parts of *today* (*this morning* or *this afternoon*), which require the Simple Past or Present Perfect tense according to the time of day we are conversing in.

> *Examples:* (11.00 a.m.). We've done a lot of work this morning, haven't we?
>
> What fine books you've brought with you this morning!
>
> (The morning is still Present Time for us.)
>
> (8.00 p.m.) We did a lot of work this morning, didn't we?
>
> What fine books you brought with you this morning!
>
> (The morning is now gone and is now part of Past Time.)

EXERCISE 54.   Elementary

Note: **Past Tense.** Whenever a new verb is learnt, the past tense and past participle should be learnt at the same time. The following exercise contains 75 very common verbs to use in the past tense; about 60 of them are irregular (strong) verbs.

Read the following sentences (a) in the Past Tense; (b) as Past Tense negatives; (c) as Past Tense questions:

1. I break a cup.
2. It begins to rain.
3. You cut your finger.
4. She comes early.
5. I lie on the bed.
6. He teaches English.
7. The river flows to the sea.
8. I know his name.
9. You lie to me.
10. The prisoner runs away.
11. He tears his coat.
12. They have a car.
13. We wake up at seven.
14. Your dog bites me.
15. It costs a lot of money.
16. You hide the key.
17. The river freezes in winter.
18. They drink tea every day.
19. I choose a book.
20. The servant sweeps the room.
21. He does his work well.
22. That pudding smells nice.
23. You find your bag.
24. You wear a lovely dress.
25. I say "No."
26. Someone steals the money.
27. We ring the bell.
28. You ride a bicycle.
29. The boy throws a ball.
30. The girl catches it.
31. I put the book on the table.
32. Mother makes a cup of tea.
33. She takes a plate from the cupboard.
34. You spend too much money.
35. She tells us a story.
36. The red light means "stop".
37. The little boy falls down.
38. They build a house.
39. The sick man gets better.
40. I eat my lunch quickly.
41. Flowers grow in my garden.
42. We buy meat.
43. He feeds his horse.
44. She loses her way.
45. We swim in the sea.
46. She understands everything.
47. The wind blows strongly.
48. We go out every day.
49. The picture hangs on the wall.
50. Her knee hurts her.
51. I use my car every day.
52. We keep our handkerchiefs in the drawer.
53. They meet outside the cinema.

54. He always pays the bill.
55. He smokes a pipe after supper.
56. She shuts the door softly.
57. The artist draws a picture.
58. The servant lights the fire every morning.
59. You hear a noise.
60. The little boy stands on a chair.
61. He leaves at six.
62. The plane flies high.
63. He tries to help them.
64. The soldiers fight the enemy.
65. She wants coffee for breakfast.
66. He sells foreign stamps.
67. The room holds 50 people.
68. He sees the film again.
69. He thinks about it.
70. They fall ill.
71. He plays football every week.
72. They write to you.
73. He reads the paper before he goes to bed.
74. He sits at the head of the table.
75. She lets them pay later.

EXERCISE 55. Elementary

Note: **Past Tense.** The word **ago** is always associated with this tense in the same way that **since** and **for** are with the Present Perfect. The word **ago** points to a date or period of time measured back from the present.

> *Examples:* I have known him since I was a boy. (=from that time up to now inclusive)
> I met him ten years ago. (=action at that time)
> I haven't played chess for four years.
> I didn't play chess four years ago.

Put the verbs into the correct tense:

1. Columbus (discover) America more than 400 years ago.
2. I (not see) you for more than a week.
3. Since when (you know) him?
4. How long ago (be) the last war?
5. They (come) here a month ago.
6. He (not speak) to me for over three weeks.

7. How long ago (you arrive) here?
8. We (finish) our supper half an hour ago.
9. She (not have) a holiday for four years.
10. I (not play) the violin since I was a little boy.
11. They (visit) Westminster Abbey a few days ago.
12. My brother (not write) to me for months.
13. I (not see) you since we met a year ago.
14. My youngest brother (get) a new job a week ago.
15. I (buy) one like it a month ago.

EXERCISE 56.   Elementary

Note: **Past Continuous Tense.** For describing actions one after another, as in a story, we put our verbs into the Past Simple Tense.

> *Example:* I **met** him when he **crossed** the street, and **then walked** home with him. (The three actions happened consecutively.)

If we want to talk about some past act that is completed while another action is still going on, we use the Past Continuous for the longer unfinished action, and the Past Simple for the shorter completed action.

> *Example:* I **met** him when he **was crossing** the street.
> (I met him in the middle of the street; after the meeting he continued to cross the street.)
> I **was going** to school when I **met** him. (I was on my way to school when this action took place.)

Do not forget to use the unstressed (weak) forms of was [wəz] and were [wə] in the affirmative:

> He was resting all the afternoon.   [wəz 'restiŋ]

Put the verbs into the Past Continuous form:

1. I (read) a book when he came in.
2. The sun (shine) when we went out.
3. When you came in I (write).
4. I came in while he (write).
5. It (rain) this morning when I got up.
6. He (work) all day yesterday.
7. When I arrived at his house he still (sleep).

8. The boy jumped off the tram while it (move).
9. The fire still (burn) at six o'clock this morning.
10. He (walk) across the bridge when his hat blew off.

No. 10

11. She cut her finger while she (cut) the bread and butter.
12. The bus started while I (get) on.
13. The light went out while we (have) supper.
14. The children (do) their homework when their father came back from the office.
15. I took another cake when you (not look)!

EXERCISE 57. Elementary and Intermediate

Note: **Past Continuous Tense.** Sometimes we use only this tense in a sentence; e.g. *While I was doing my homework, he was reading a book.* Such a sentence merely tells us that the two actions were taking place at the same time, but says nothing of their beginning or end. We are not interested in the completion of either action, only in the activities themselves.

Do not forget that certain verbs (see Exercise 49) are not usually found in Continuous forms of tenses.

Put the verbs into the correct form of the Past Tense (Simple or Continuous):

1. He (sit) in a café when I (see) him.
2. When I (go) out the sun (shine).
3. The boy (fall down) while he (run).
4. When the war (begin) we (live) in London.

5. The light (go out) while I (have) tea.
6. I (have) tea when the light (go out).
7. My friends (sing) when I (come) into the room.
8. While you (play) the piano I (write) a letter.
9. When I (be) at school I (learn) Latin. ("To be" has no continuous form.)
10. He (eat) his dinner when I (go) to see him.
11. You (wear) your new hat when I (meet) you yesterday.
12. When I (have) a dog I always (take) him out for a walk in the evening.
13. When the phone (ring), I (have) a bath.
14. Large crowds (wait) at the station when the Prime Minister (arrive).
15. I (speak) to her several times, but she (read) and (not hear) me.
16. We (walk) to the station when the storm (break).
17. We (run) under a bridge when the storm (break). (*Think carefully what this sentence means!*)
18. When the teacher (come) in, the boys (play).
19. He (eat) three sandwiches while you (talk) to him.
20. While he (write) a letter, the telephone (ring); as he (go) to answer it, he (hear) a knock at the door; the telephone still (ring) while he (walk) to the door, but just as he (open) it, it (stop).

EXERCISE 58. Intermediate

Note: **Past Tenses** (Simple and Continuous). See Exercises 56 and 57.

Put the verbs into the correct form of the Past Tense (Simple, or Continuous):

We (enter) Port Said harbour when I (come) on deck. As soon as our ship (come) near enough, a large number of boats (set out) from the shore. We could see that they (bring) money-changers, guides, and men selling all the wonderful things of the East. While I (leave) the ship I (notice) that the rest of the passengers (argue) about the prices in loud voices. I (walk) about for an hour and (watch) the gay street life; men (sell) strange fruits and vegetables, and tradesmen (mend) shoes or (make) carpets in their little shops. I (return) to my ship as the sun (set); the "market" on the ship still (continue). An old man who (sit) on the deck (offer) me a beautiful Persian rug for only £10. I (talk) hard for ten minutes, and just as the ship (go) I (buy) it for £1. As I (go) to my cabin I (see) a sailor with a rug like mine. I (ask) him the price. "Twenty-five pence," he said, "but I (pay) too much for it. A man that I (talk) to just now only (pay) ten pence." As I (undress) that night, I (notice) a little piece of cloth which (hang) from one corner of my rug. On it were the words "Made in Manchester."

EXERCISE 59. Elementary

Note: **Revision of Present, Past and Present Perfect Tenses.** Remember the type of adverb associated with each of these tenses:

(a) **Present.** General time notions (frequency, habit).
(*Sometimes, generally, always, normally, nowadays.*)

(b) **Present Perfect.** Adverbs of frequency as for Present Tense (answering the question "How often?"); all expressions meaning "up to now" or "finished by now".
(*Always, never, often, seldom, sometimes,* etc.
Since . . ., for . . ., already, just, (not) yet, this week, month, etc.)

(c) **Past.** Adverbs indicating a date, or period in the past.
(*Yesterday, last week, month,* etc., *in 1950,* etc.)

Read the following sentences:

(a) *in the Present Perfect tense, without making any other changes;*

(b) *in the Past Tense, using the time-adverb given at the end instead of the adverb in* **bold type**:

Example: I **always** have cocoa for supper. (last night)
    (a) I *have* always *had* cocoa for supper.
    (b) I *had* cocoa for supper *last night.*

1. I **always** drink tea for breakfast (yesterday).
2. The class **usually** begins at six o'clock (last year).
3. His brother **always** lives in Cairo (in 1930).

4. We **sometimes** go to Port Said (for our last holiday).
5. It **never** rains here (last week).
6. Mr. Y **never** pays his bills (last month).
7. He **often** makes himself ill with ice-cream (yesterday).
8. The aeroplane **always** starts very early (this morning).
9. It **usually** arrives in the afternoon (when you were out).
10. He **never** smokes in bed (when he was ill).
11. She **generally** makes mistakes (when she was at school).
12. These children **often** lose their pencils (at school).
13. Do you **often** write letters (while you were on holiday)?
14. Do you **ever** play football (when you were a boy)?
15. Does the train **ever** start at the right time (before the war)?
16. Does John **always** forget his books (yesterday)?
17. Do you **always** have coffee after dinner (at the Smiths')?
18. He **sometimes** sleeps in the garden (last night).
19. We don't **often** see a black horse (all last week).
20. That student doesn't **always** come (last Wednesday).

EXERCISE 60. **Intermediate**

Note: **Revision.** (See previous exercise.)

Read each of the following sentences twice, incorporating the given time-adverbs (a) *and* (b) *instead of the adverb* **in bold type:**

> *Example:* John was learning English **when I went to see him yesterday;** (*a*) at this very moment, too; (*b*) for the last six months.
>
> (*a*) John *is learning* English at this very moment, too.
> (*b*) John *has been learning* English for the last six months.

(*Keep the same form of the tense of the given sentence* (*simple or continuous*) *in the other two.*)

1. We are living in the country **now:** (a) until the war; (b) since the war.
2. The fat lady next door **frequently** practises singing: (a) for three hours yesterday; (b) every day since **we** came to live here.

No. 3

3. He was preparing for the examination **last month**: (a) now; (b) for the last fortnight.
4. I've known all about it **for years**: (a) at last; (b) **days ago.**
5. I was selling a lot of my old books **last month**: (a) **today**; (b) lately.
6. You don't often come to see us **nowadays**: (a) last year; (b) since you left the district.
7. Who are you laughing at **now**?: (a) just now; (b) **all** this time.
8. **Then** she had to go to the doctor's: (a) in a minute; (b) every morning this week.
9. He has told me that **time and time again**: (a) two years ago; (b) every time he sees me.
10. She **always** keeps us waiting a long time: (a) last night; (b) this evening.

EXERCISE 61.   Elementary and Intermediate

Note: **Revision.**   (See Exercise 59.)

Put the verbs into the correct tense (Present, Past or Present Perfect):

1. She (go) away every week-end.
2. He (go) abroad last week.
3. No, he isn't here.   He just (go) out.
4. He (go) downstairs when I (meet) him.

5. "Where is Mr. Green?" "He (go) out ten minutes ago."
6. This boy never (see) the sea.
7. You (see) my bag? I (lose) it.
8. I (see) you yesterday. You (sit) outside a café.
9. He (already write) a lot of letters, but his sister (not write) many.
10. He is busy now; he (write) a letter.
11. I (hope) he (get) better now, I (hear) he (have) a bad cold all the week.
12. You (see) a good film lately?
13. He (live) in England since 1938.
14. When I last (see) him, he (live) in London.
15. He (sit) in the garden when the storm (break).
16. I (hear) the news last night, but I (not hear) it today.
17. When I (see) him, he (sit) asleep in a chair.

No. 17

18. John (write) a letter now.
19. He already (write) two letters this morning.
20. He (write) a lot of letters yesterday.
21. We (not play) tennis together since last May.
22. I (learn) English for the last two years, but now I (study) Russian, too.
23. Lend me your rubber. (*Amer.* eraser). I (make) a mistake and (wish) to rub it out.
24. "What you (look for)?"
    "I (lose) my purse near here and (want) to find it before it (get) dark."
    "When you (lose) it?"
    "I think that I (drop) it when I (go) to school this morning."
25. ?"You (remember) my name, or you (forget) it?"

EXERCISE 62. Elementary

Note: **Future Tense.** The pattern for the Simple Future tense is:

I/we shall (will)[1] go.
He *etc.*/you/they will go.

Shall I/we go?
Will he *etc.*/you they go?

I/we shall (will)[1] not go. (shan't/won't)
He *etc.*/you/they will not (won't) go.

A possible confusion in modern English (the meaning of "Will you?") is discussed and practised in Exercises 68 and 69).

Notice that in spoken English WILL is a convenient form to use, as it can be shortened to . . . 'll for all persons:

I, you, he, *etc.*, we, they/'ll go.

Put the following sentences into the Simple Future tense:

1. We always ask that question.
2. You never answer me correctly without the help of the book.
3. I never believe you.
4. You don't understand it.
5. It doesn't cost very much.
6. We don't do any homework in the class.
7. Why doesn't she drink her cocoa?
8. I eat an orange every day.
9. I never have much money.
10. It doesn't hurt you.
11. I know the answer now. (Tomorrow . . .)
12. He can swim. (After six lessons . . .)
13. You must work harder.
14. I must read more books.
15. He doesn't like it at all.
16. Do I forget so easily?
17. They come here every day.

[1] The form with WILL for all persons is more usual in American and Scottish English than British English. In B.E. it is rare with many of the verbs of Ex. 49 (but see also Ex. 65); SHALL is normal in questions. Some Scottish speakers seldom use SHALL even for questions in the 1st person.

18. I don't remember his name.
19. I feel ill if I eat too much.
20. Do we need any new books?

EXERCISE 63.   Elementary and Intermediate

Note: **The Future Tense** (with added meaning). The forms in the previous exercise describe the idea of future time only. By reversing the pattern of SHALL/WILL to

> I/we will go.
> He, *etc.* /you/they shall go.

we add something of the speaker's attitude towards this future act.

Will used with the first person colours the pure future time with the speaker's **intention** or **promise.**

> I will (I'll) give you a new book tomorrow.
> (*I promise to give you . . .*)
>
> I will (I'll) ask the director myself.
> (*I mean (intend) to ask him . . .*)
>
> I won't forget what you've told me.
> (*I promise not to . . .*)

Shall used with the other persons colours the pure future time with a feeling of the speaker's **promise** or **insistence** (*affirmative*), **restraint** or **prohibition** (*negative*).

> You shall have it back tomorrow.
> (*I promise to give it to you.*)
>
> You shan't leave till you promise to come again.
> (*I don't allow you to leave, I forbid you to leave . . .*)
>
> I'll begin again, and you shan't stop me this time.
> (*I intend to . . . and you are not to stop . . .*)
>
>   Notice also the use of WILL (=to be willing) in polite requests:
>
> If you will wait a moment, I'll fetch you a chair.
> (*If you are willing to . . .*)

We can call the SHALL/WILL forms of Exercise 62 **the Plain** or **Ordinary** Future; and the W./SH. forms of this exercise the **Coloured** Future.

*Complete the following Coloured Future sentences with "**shall**" or "**will**":*

1. I ... pay you next week.
2. You ... have a watch for your twentyfirst birthday.
3. Whoever broke it ... pay for it!
4. After such bad behaviour he ... n't come again.
5. You ... have a piece of chocolate if you're good.
6. If you ... look after the luggage, I ... buy the tickets.
7. You ... not go until I know the truth.
8. "... you have tea or coffee?"
   "I ... have some tea, please."
9. In that case *Tom* . . . have what he asks for, but *you* ... n't.
10. ... you lend me ten pence? I ... pay you back tomorrow.
11. You ... have a bicycle of your own when you are older.
12. Who ... say whether the doctor was right or wrong?
13. You ... n't take it away from him, I ... n't allow you to.
14. I ... crack the nuts, and you ... eat them.
15. "With rings on her fingers and bells on her toes,
    She ... have music wherever she goes."

    (Old Children's Rhyme.)

EXERCISE 64. Elementary

Note: **The Future Tense (GOING-TO).**

Another common way of expressing future time is the use of **going to** with an infinitive. It is an easier pattern to use than **shall/will,** but it normally means that the subject intends the action, or that the speaker feels that the action is certain to happen. We could call this the **Intended Future** or the **Future of Intention.**

> *Examples:* I'm going to study English. (*subject's intention*)
> Our teacher is going to read to us. (*subject's intention*)
> Now you're going to hear me sing! (*speaker's certainty*)
> Look! The sun's going to shine in a minute. (*speaker's certainty*)

Very often it makes little difference to our meaning if we choose either *shall/will* or *going-to*. (See Exercise 65 for examples where one of the two forms is not possible.)

Change the following future tenses into the "going-to" form:

1. He will leave tomorrow.
2. Where will he stay?
3. John will wait for us there.
4. We shall write letters all the afternoon.
5. He will lend me the money.
6. We shall eat them all.
7. My father will build a new house.
8. I'm afraid it will cost a lot of money.
9. They will grow beans in their garden.
10. Mr. Thompson will sell his house.
11. We'll work harder next year.
12. He'll speak to us about it.
13. I shall have three weeks' holiday this year.
14. They will learn Russian.
15. I think I shall be sick.

EXERCISE 65. Intermediate and Advanced

Note: **Shall/will** and **Going-to** (Future Tense).

The following pairs of sentences show that the *shall/will* and *going-to* forms of the future tense are not always interchangeable. The bracketed examples are not possible.

1. She will know in a minute.
   (She is going to know in a minute.)

2. I shall understand it better tomorrow.
   (I'm going to understand it better tomorrow.)

3. He'll give it to you if you ask him.
   (He is going to give it to you if you ask him.)

4. Sometimes the baby will cry for hours.
   (Sometimes the baby is going to cry for hours.)

1 and 2 are verbs describing mental states and so have nothing to do with the *intention* of the speaker. The future tense of 3

depends on a Condition, and so is independent of the subject's intention. The fourth example uses *will* in an idiomatic way that expresses Habit; *going-to* cannot replace it in this sense.

Compare also the last sentence of Exercise 64 with ones that demand *shall/will:*

I think I'm going to be sick. (*Speaker's certainty.*)

I think I'll have a glass of water. (*Speaker's intention: the Coloured Future.*)

I think I shall know the answer tomorrow. (*Plain Future.*)

In most cases, fortunately, either pattern can be used, but not of course with the same shade of meaning. This next exercise practises both forms.

Read the following sentences twice in the future:

    (a) *in* shall/will *form,*

    (b) *in* going-to *form,*

in each case replacing the time expression (**in bold type**) *by the future time adverb "tomorrow":*

1. The servant cleaned my room **yesterday**.
2. We've **already** climbed the mountain.
3. They came here **last year**, didn't they?
4. It didn't cost so much **a week ago**.
5. He cut you a bigger piece of cake **last time**.
6. They didn't do any business with us **in 1935**.
7. Prices have gone up **during the last few weeks**.
8. Did he take you with him to the Zoo **last time**?
9. I have been very busy **today**.
10. He had a tooth pulled out **yesterday**.
11. He looked for you at the party **last night**.
12. He saw the queen **three days ago**.
13. We took our examinations **in 1940**.
14. Did we go out **yesterday afternoon**?
15. He stayed home **till six o'clock**.
16. They haven't paid me **since March**.
17. Have you written to him **since**?
18. We didn't have time to see them all.
19. John remembered your name **yesterday**.
20. Mary knew the answer to this question **before**.

Comments on Exercise 65. The last two sentences are not very probable in the *going-to* form. This is because "know" and "remember" belong to that class of "automatic" verbs describing mental and emotional states; *going-to* colours the future with the subject's intention, and it is not very logical to imply this with acts or states over which we have no physical control. (All verbs in this class also belong to the group mentioned in Exercise 49.)

The note to Exercise 49 showed the use of the Present Continuous tense to express the **Arranged Future.** Most of the sentences in Exercise 65 (but not the last two) can be put into this form, too, with a rather different meaning. For example:

5.	He is going to cut . . .	(He tells me so.)
	He is cutting . . .	(I've told him to; arranged it for you.)
12.	He is going to see . . .	(He has decided to watch the procession, perhaps.)
	He is seeing the queen . . .	(An appointment has been arranged.)

EXERCISE 66. Elementary

Note: **Present Continuous as Future.**

Examples of this usage are given in the note to Exercise 49, where we suggested it might be called the **Arranged Future.** It is most commonly found with verbs of movement, nearly always has a *personal* subject, and cannot be made with verbs that are not found in Continuous tense forms (*see list after Exercise 49.*)

Read the following sentences using the Present Continuous Tense:

1. We shall start strong verbs on Monday.
2. He'll come to see me the day after tomorrow.
3. We shall set out at two o'clock.
4. She will invite seven other people.
5. Will you stay at home tonight?
6. I'll play tennis this afternoon.
7. He will use it again tomorrow.
8. The children will have cakes for tea today.
9. She will leave by the three o'clock train.
10. He'll give us a new one next week.

11. I shall take the examination on Friday.
12. She will sing a group of songs next.
13. We shall go out at seven.
14. We shall return tomorrow afternoon.
15. He will sail for India on Friday.

EXERCISE 67. Elementary

Note: **The Future Continuous.** In its simplest form this tense is used in the same way as the Past and Present Continuous tenses; that is, it describes an action *in progress* at some future moment.

When I arrived, they were having supper.

They are having supper now.

They'll be having supper when we get there after the concert.

(*Verbs of the type listed after Exercise 49 are not used in this tense.*)

Using the adverbs between brackets, read the following sentences in the future:

1. What are you doing (in ten years' time)?
2. He is sleeping (at four o'clock).
3. She is doing her homework (after supper).
4. It's raining (when you come back).
5. I'm still mending the chair (at seven o'clock).
6. She is talking (for at least another three hours).
7. I'm waiting for you (at the usual time).
8. We're listening to you (at the concert).
9. She's making tea (about then).
10. He's travelling (all night).
11. I'm doing the washing (tomorrow morning).
12. They're studying English (for two more years).
13. He's writing to her (next week).
14. You're swimming in the sea (this time next week).
15. We're working very hard (in the autumn).

EXERCISE 68. Elementary and Intermediate

Note: **The Future Continuous.** Like the Present Continuous in Exercise 66, the Future Continuous can be used in the same way to express a definite or fixed future. *Going-to* can replace either of them when it means the *speaker's certainty*.

There is no important difference of meaning between the uses of these two Continuous tenses for expressing a definite future, but they are sometimes found together in the same sentence (or two adjacent sentences), where the Future Continuous will be used for something a little more remote or a little less definite than the Present Continuous.

Examples: He's *playing* a violin solo next, and he'*ll be playing* some more later on.

We'*re going* to school for another term and then we'*ll be going* to the University.

Re-state the following, using the Future Continuous form:

1. I'm seeing him tomorrow.
2. They're going to do it again later.
3. He is leaving in a few days.
4. The leaves are going to fall soon.
5. I'll write to you later.
6. He's going to meet us at the station.
7. We're going to have crab for supper.
8. They are going to town again this week.
9. We're having coffee after dinner as usual.
10. He's coming home soon.
11. We are having dinner in half an hour.
12. I shall see her tomorrow afternoon.
13. You're going to learn more about this tense next lesson.
14. Hurry up! the train is leaving in a minute.
15. You'll forget your head next, you absent-minded old thing!

EXERCISE 69. Elementary and Intermediate

Note: **Future Tense** (questions in the 2nd person).

The Plain Future forms of Exercise 62 have a confusion in the form **Will you?** It is not always clear in modern English whether this is a Plain Future question or a Request.

Will you visit him tomorrow? may mean:

(a) Please visit him tomorrow. (*Request.*)

(b) Will your programme tomorrow include (by chance) a visit to this person? (*Plain Future question.*)

In classical English the Plain Future question was **Shall you?** (still included in some grammars); and the Request was **Will you?** Unfortunately the form: *Shall you visit him tomorrow?* (=in the course of your day's activities) is no longer current English, and the form **Will you?** usually serves both purposes.

In this century there has been increasing use of the *Future Continuous* to replace the now dead **Shall you?**

So the classical: *Shall you visit him tomorrow?*

is heard now as: *Will you be visiting him tomorrow?*

This use of the Future Continuous is now the usual form of Plain Future question in the 2nd person whenever it is felt necessary to avoid any confusion with a Request.

Use the Future Continuous tense in the following sentences to make it clear that they are not requests:

1. Will you come again soon?
2. Will you give us another lecture?
3. What will you have to drink?
4. Will you post the letters tomorrow?
5. Will you go away from here?
6. Will you have the next lesson on Friday?
7. Will you have lunch in town?
8. Will you sleep here tonight?
9. Will you stay with us when you get back?
10. Will you take your friend to the theatre?

No. 11

11. Will you make another cake like this?
12. Will you buy a newspaper when you go out?
13. Will you ask him for some more money?

14. Will you sell him your radio?
15. Will you sing another song?

EXERCISE 70. Intermediate

Note: **Future Tense** (questions in the 2nd person).
(See notes to previous exercise.)

Compare these two forms:
(*a*) Will you (please) come tomorrow? (*Request.*)
(*b*) Will you be coming tomorrow? (*No request; asking about your future activities.*)

Make questions from the following sentences in two ways:
(a) *as a request*; (b) *as a polite query about the statement* (*Plain Future question, 2nd person*):

Example: See him tomorrow.
(*a*) Will you (please) see him tomorrow?
(*b*) Will you be seeing him tomorrow?

1. Come to see me soon.
2. Arrange (fix) the meeting tomorrow.
3. Use the big spoon.
4. Have an early breakfast.
5. Have the desks painted! (Causative.)
6. Do it again.
7. Make all the arrangements.
8. Write the dictation on the blackboard.
9. Give us an examination.
10. Keep the books in the cupboard.
11. Light a fire in the sitting-room.
12. Write to him again.
13. Go to the office on your way home.
14. Make some more coffee.
15. Give us another homework.

EXERCISE 71. Elementary and Intermediate

Note: **Future Substitutes.**
Other verbs of intention, promise, prohibition, etc., are often used instead of *shall/will* or *going-to*. The Coloured Future (*will/*

shall) forms are most often expressed in some other way, as this pattern is felt to be rather literary and a little stiff. Some of the commonest substitutes are suggested in this next exercise.

Use the given verbs instead of the **shall/will** *forms so that the new sentences express the same ideas as the originals:*

> *Example:* I will take the exam. in June (intend); won't you take it at the same time? (want)
>
> I intend to take . . .; don't you want to take it . . . ?

1. Will you have some more cake? (like)
2. Shall I get you another book? (want)
3. What will you do now? (mean)
4. You shall stay here till I come back. (is to)
5. We won't listen to him. (choose)
6. I'll be going next week. (intend)
7. I won't do what you tell me. (refuse)
8. You shall have a new bicycle. (promise)
9. I won't take up any more of your time. (want)
10. We'll make our presence known to him. (mean)
11. I think I shall go away next week-end. (hope)
12. He says he will get a rise next month. (expect)
13. They won't accept your apology. (refuse)
14. John will sit for the examination. (intend)
15. You shan't leave without saying 'hello' to him. (is to)
    (*No. 8 should be changed into the passive voice.*)

EXERCISE 72. Elementary

Note: **No Future Tense with time conjunctions.**

Some sentences are composed of a **Main Clause** and one or more **Subsidiary Clauses.** The Main Clause can stand alone; the other clauses only make sense with the Main Clause.

Although he is a clever student, **he doesn't work hard** *when* he is at school.

The Main Clause is in **bold type;** it makes complete sense without the rest of the sentence. The other two clauses (beginning with the conjunctions (= joining words) *although* and *when*) do not make complete sense without the Main Clause. The word *when* here is a Temporal (= time) Conjunction; it introduces a Temporal (= time) Clause:

Even if the general time sense of a sentence is future, we do not use a Future Tense after a Time Conjunction.

Examples: I'll ask him *before* he **leaves**.

He'll pay you *as soon* as he **gets** the money.

The chief conjunctions of time are:

when, until *(till), before, after, as soon (long) as, while, by the time (that).*

Notice the tenses used in the two clauses of each of the following sentences and put in suitable conjunctions of time:

1. He will stay here ... you come.
2. I'll come and see you ... I have time.
3. We shall be ready ... you are.
4. ... you come tomorrow, I will give you a new book.
5. ... they show me their homework, I will correct it.
6. We shall go ... he is ready.
7. She will speak to you ... you come in.
8. You must wait ... the light changes to green.

No. 8

9. I'll write to you ... I leave England.
10. Let's stay at home ... the rain stops.
11. These brave men will fight ... they die.
12. ... I live, I shall always remember his face.
13. You will be able to play the piano ... you like.
14. They will not climb the hill ... the moon rises.
15. Don't buy bananas ... they become cheaper.

16.   We must buy some shirts ... they become dearer.
17.   This coat will lose its colour ... it's washed.
18.   He will sell the cloth ... the price rises.
19.   I shall wait ... the price falls.
20.   The corn will grow quickly ... they water the fields.

EXERCISE 73.   Elementary and Intermediate

Note: **The Future Perfect Tense.**

Just as the Present Perfect tells us about an act that is complete *now*, so the Future Perfect tells us about an act that will be finished *by a certain future date.*

Just as the Present Perfect does not tell us **when** the action *took place*, so the Future Perfect does not tell us **when** the action *will take place.* We use "simple" tenses (past or future) for these dates.

Look at the following pairs of sentences:

I've read three of Shaw's plays. (I *know* about them **now**.)
I shall have read six of Shaw's plays by the end of the year (I *shall know* about them **then**.)

I had my supper an hour ago. (*action at known time*)
I've had my supper (already). (*finished by now*)

I shall have my supper at 7 o'clock. (*action at known future time*)
I shall have had my supper by the time you come. (*finished by then*)

There is also a **Future Perfect Continuous Tense**, but it is not often used.

Example: By next month *he'll have been teaching* at this school for ten years. (= and will probably continue to teach there)

Notice how **by** often introduces the future perfect:
I shall read it next week/*on* Monday/*in* the evening/*at* 2 o'clock.
I shall have read it *by* next week/Monday/the evening/2 o'clock.

Put the verbs into the correct form of the Future Perfect Tense:

1.   By next June he (write) his second novel.
2.   Before his next visit here he (return) from a world tour.
3.   Before you go to see them, they (leave) the country.
4.   He (finish) this work before you leave.
5.   By the end of the summer he (teach) us to speak English.

6. When you come back he already (buy) the house.
7. The meeting (finish) by the time we get there.
8. By next month he (sell) all his furniture.
9. By next Sunday you (stay) with us for five weeks.
10. He (take) his examination by his next birthday.
11. I hope, when you have finished this exercise, you (not make) many mistakes in it.
12. I hope it (stop) raining by five o'clock.
13. I (finish) long before you get back.
14. If we don't get there before seven, they (eat and drink) everything.
15. I hope you (not forget) all this by tomorrow!

EXERCISE 74. Intermediate

Note: No future Perfect Tense with time conjunctions. (See Exercise 72.) Where this tense might be expected in a time clause, we find the *Present* Perfect Tense instead.

You *will have finished* your work by six o'clock.

I'll stay until you *have finished* your work.

Put the verbs into the correct tense:

1. I'll wait here until you (write) the letter.
2. Don't come until I (finish) lunch.
3. You needn't bring the book back until you (read) it.
4. Perhaps I'll know the language after I (live) here for five years.
5. After the winter rain (fall), the rivers will begin to rise.
6. Don't borrow any more books until you (read) these.
7. Shall I be able to read a newspaper when I (learn) a thousand English words?
8. I won't give you another homework till you (finish) your corrections.
9. You will know your way round the town better when you (be) here a little longer.
10. They won't return home until they (see) the whole country.
11. When you (rest), I'll take you round the garden.

THE VERB

12. As soon as I (save) £1,000, I'll buy a car.
13. They won't send the goods till you (pay) for them.
14. Bring it back when you (finish) with it.
15. Show it to me as soon as you (unpack) it.

EXERCISE 75. Elementary

Note: **The Past Perfect Tense.** This tense bears the same relation to *past* time as the *Present* Perfect does to *now*, and the *Future* Perfect to *future time*; that is, it describes an action completed before the past moment we are talking about.

I've read three of Shaw's plays. (I *know* about them **now**.)
I shall have read six of his plays by the end of the year.
    (I *shall know* about them **then**.)
I **had read** "Pygmalion" before I saw it on the stage.
    (I *knew* the play **at that time**.)
I **had seen** "Pygmalion" on the stage before I read it.
    (I saw it first, then read it.)

This tense (like the Future Perfect) is often associated with Time Clauses.

Put the verbs into the correct form (Past or Past Perfect):

1. She told me his name after he (leave).
2. He (do) nothing before he saw me.
3. My friend enjoyed his food as soon as he (taste) it.
4. He thanked me for what I (do).
5. I (be) sorry that I had hurt him.
6. After they had gone, I (sit) down and (rest).
7. Did you post the letter after you (write) it?
8. As soon as you (go), I wanted to see you again.
9. They dressed after they (wash).
10. After I had heard the news, I (hurry) to see him.
11. She told me her name after I (ask) her twice.
12. Before we (go) very far, we found that we (lose) our way.
13. After you (go), I went to sleep. *had gone, went*
14. I read the book after I (finish) my work.
15. When we arrived, the dinner already (begin).

had already begun

EXERCISE 76. Elementary and Intermediate

Note: **The Past Perfect Tense.**

One of the commonest uses of this tense is in **Reported Speech.**
If we begin "He **said** that ... ", *etc.*, the report that follows must
all be finished by that past moment (*he said*). So the words:

"I saw him" must be reported as "He said that he had seen him."

Put the verbs into the correct form (Past or Past Perfect):

1. They (go) home after they (finish) their work.
2. She said that she already (see) the Pyramids.
3. She just (go) out when I called at her house.
4. They told him they (not meet) him before.
5. He asked why we (come) so early.
6. He wondered why I (not visit) him before.
7. We asked him what countries he (visit).
8. We (hear) that a fire (break out) in the neighbouring house.
9. They drank small cups of coffee after they (finish) dinner.
10. She told her teacher that her mother (help) her with her homework the previous evening, and (tell) her the words she (not know).
11. The fire (spread) to the next building before the firemen (arrive).
12. He (take) the money after I (ask) him not to do so.
13. He had already learnt English before he (leave) for England; but before he (arrive) in England, he (forget) some.
14. My friend (not see) me for many years when I (meet) him last week.
15. The sun (set) before I (be) ready to go.

EXERCISE 77. Elementary

Note: **Revision exercise for all tenses** (except conditional clauses).

Put the verbs into the correct tenses:

1. We (go) to the theatre last night.
2. He usually (write) in green ink.

3. She (play) the piano when our guests (arrive) last night.
4. We (do) an English exercise. (*How many possibilities?*)
5. She just (come) in and (see) you in five minutes.
6. I (come) as soon as my work is finished. You (be) ready?
7. Where you (go) for your holidays last year?
8. My mother (come) to stay with us next week-end.
9. I never (see) snow.
10. We (not live) in England for the last two years.
11. I (lose) my keys; I cannot remember where I last (see) them.
12. He (not arrive) when I (write) my last letter to you.
13. Whenever he (go) to town nowadays, he (spend) a lot of money.
14. I never (forget) what you just (tell) me.
15. When I last (stay) in Cairo, I (ride) to the Pyramids on a camel that my friend (borrow) the day before.
16. I (finish) the book before my next birthday.
17. He (walk) very quickly when I (meet) him yesterday.
18. He said he (be) sorry he (give) me so much trouble.
19. I (know) him for a very long time.
20. I (study) English for six years now.

CONDITIONAL CLAUSES

EXERCISE 78. Elementary

Note: Like time clauses (with *when*, *before*, etc.), clauses of condition (with *if* and *unless* mainly) have no *shall/will* or *should/would* tenses in them.

The three principal sentence patterns using **if** (or **unless**) are:

1. Main clause (future)/ "if" (present).
   He **will come** if you **call** him.
   (Something will happen after fulfilling a certain *condition*.)

2. Main clause (conditional)/ "if" (past).
   He **would come** if you **called** him.
   (This is the probable result of a certain condition that we

suppose or imagine. The "if"-clause is not taking place now, but I can imagine the probable result. We include here all the *unreal* "ifs," like "If you were a fish, the cat would eat you.")

3. Main clause (conditional perfect)/ "if" (past perfect).

He **would have come** if you **had called** him.

(But in fact he did *not* come. Why not? Because you did *not* call him. These are past conditions, and can never be realized; but we like to imagine things other than they really were. We use this form a great deal when making excuses! "I shouldn't have been late if ...," *etc.*)

The most important words for introducing a conditional clause are **if** and **unless** (= if not).

He won't come unless you call him.

Read the following sentences, notice carefully the tense of the verb in each half, and say which of the three types of condition each sentence is:

1. If I come, I shall see you.
2. You will spoil it if you aren't careful.
3. We would answer if we could.
4. They will get wet if it rains.
5. I should be pleased if you came.
6. If I had known that, I should not have made a mistake.
7. It would have been better if you had waited.
8. If I were you, I should go home immediately.
9. Will you help me if I need you?
10. He would have told you if you had asked him.
11. They would be silly if they did not take this opportunity.
12. If it is fine, I shall go for a swim.
13. If it rained, I should stay at home.
14. I'll help you if I can.
15. It would have broken if you had not caught it.
16. If you had done as I told you, you would have succeeded.
17. If you did as I told you, you would succeed.
18. You'll succeed if you do as I tell you.
19. If you are good, I'll give you a piece of chocolate.
20. You will pass your examination if you work hard.

EXERCISE 79. Elementary

Note: No. 8 of the previous exercise has the form "If I were ..."
The "if"-clauses are really in the subjunctive mood (a form of
the verb used for unreal situations), but modern English has no
distinctive form for this. It is the same as the past tense for all
verbs except "be", which still has a special form "If I/you/he,
etc., were."

*Note carefully the tenses used in the following sentences, and add
"if" or "unless" to each one:*

1. He wouldn't have waited ... you'd been late.
2. He won't speak French ... he goes to France.
3. I'll go to the door ... I hear the bell.
4. I shan't go to the door ... I hear the bell.
5. ... he wrote to me, I should write to him.
6. I shan't write to him ... he writes to me.
7. ... the clock had been right, we should have caught the train.
8. He will not learn much ... he works harder.
9. ... you send a telegram now, he'll get it this evening.
10. ... he started immediately, he would arrive by midday.
11. I should never have found the house ... the policeman hadn't helped me.
12. ... you rang, he would come.[1]
13. He would come ... you rang.
14. ... you had rung, he would have come.
15. He would have come ... you had rung.

EXERCISE 80. Elementary and Intermediate

Note: Look once more at the 3 basic types of condition, and
learn the short-forms of the helping verbs used:
1. He will come if you wait. (*He'll come ...*)
2. He would come if you waited. (*He'd come ...*)
3. He would have come if you had waited. (*He'd have come if you'd waited.*)

[1] In the last four sentences the normal spoken English short-forms
(he would = he'd, and he had = he'd) have been omitted to avoid
confusion at this early stage. The teacher might, however, read them
to the students with these contractions.

Read each of the following sentences, then say (or write) it in the other two types of condition:

1. He'll come if you wait.
2. If you ring the bell, the servant will come.
3. You'll catch the train if you take a taxi.
4. If he wrote to me, I should write to him.
5. You would have found the book if you had opened the bag.
6. If he saw you, he would speak to you.
7. The streets would be wet if it rained.
8. You'll be ill if you drink that water.
9. What will you do if you meet Mr. Robinson?
10. I shouldn't have spoken to him even if he had spoken to me.
11. If a beggar asks you for money, will you give him any?
12. What would happen if the bridge broke?

No. 12

13. If he had fallen into the river, he would have been drowned.
14. If he had been able to swim, he wouldn't have been drowned.
15. If you buy that big house, you will need several servants.
16. Will you be angry if I steal your pocket-knife?
17. If he'd been thirsty, he would have drunk some water.
18. I shall come and see you if I have time.
19. If you put the parcel on the table, the boy will post it for you.

20. If you could come it would be very nice.
21. It would have been better if they hadn't come.
22. I'll give it to you if you must have one.
23. He'll certainly do it if it's possible.
24. If you go to town, will you buy something for me?
25. We shall be pleased if our school wins the match.

EXERCISE 81.   Elementary

Note: Revision material for Exercises 78–80.

Read the following sentences with the verbs in the correct tenses:

1. You will be ill if you (eat) so much.
2. I (go) if I had known.
3. If my car not (break) down, I should have caught the train.
4. If she were older, she (have) more sense.
5. If you (read) that book carefully, you would understand it.
6. If the children (be) good, they can stay up late.
7. I (buy) that hat if it were not so dear.
8. You (kill) yourself if you always work as hard as that.
9. If they had waited, they (find) me.
10. I'm sure she will do well if she (go) to the University.
11. If it (be) fine tomorrow, I shall play tennis.
12. I shouldn't have thought it possible unless I (see) it.
13. We (enjoy) the play better if it had not been so long.
14. They would do it if they (can).
15. If dinner is not ready, I (go) without it.
16. If he wants to play the violin, I (play) the piano for him.
17. The dog (bite) you if it had not been tied up.
18. If you don't shut that window, we all (catch) cold.
19. The child (be killed) if the train hadn't stopped quickly.
20. I should have come yesterday if I (have) nothing to do.

EXERCISE 82.   Elementary and Intermediate

Note: More advanced revision of Exercises 78–80.

Complete the following sentences:

1. You will get into trouble if ...

D

2.   Your dress would look better if ...
3.   Don't give him anything unless ...
4.   If I had time, ...
5.   If it hadn't been raining, ...
6.   I might have learnt more English if ...
7.   The teacher would not be angry with you if ...
8.   You will lose your money if ...
9.   Flowers will not grow well unless ...
10. A violinist must practise if ...
11. You could live more cheaply if ...
12. I don't like tea unless ...
13. I should have won the prize if ...
14. The soup will get cold unless ...
15. You would be ill if ...
16. I cannot wake at six o'clock unless ...
17. She will play the piano for you if ...
18. My friend would have helped you if ...
19. The photograph would have been better if ...
20. If I had plenty of money, ...
21. Get ready quickly if ...
22. I don't like meat unless ...
23. If you had worked harder, ...
24. Why didn't you do it if ...
25. He won't come unless ...
26. I shouldn't have lost my money if ...
27. You would be very angry with us if ...
28. If I were you, ...
29. If I had known he was here, ...
30. We shall be very disappointed if ...

EXERCISE 83.   Intermediate

Note: **Type 3 condition with inversion.**

It does not matter which of the two clauses of a Conditional
sentence stands first. A comma usually separates the clauses when
the "if"–clause stands first.

You would have seen him if you had come earlier.
If you had come earlier, you would have seen him.

This 3rd type of conditional sentence can also be expressed by omitting the word "if" and using the order of a question. (Inversion of verb and subject.)

Had you come earlier, you would have seen him.

The clause of condition usually stands first in this pattern.

It is a literary form and is more often seen in print than heard as part of the spoken language.

Re-word the following conditional sentences in the inversion form:

1. If you had come later, you would have missed the train.
2. If they had known before, they would have accepted the invitation.
3. If he had taken proper care, he would not have lost his way.
4. If we had arrived later, we should have found every hotel full.
5. If we had heard of you before, we should certainly have come to see you.
6. If it had not been a fine day, we should have stayed at home.
7. If there had been time, he would have shown us over the castle.
8. If you had wanted to, you could have stayed for a meal.
9. If we had thought of it before, we could have asked the others to meet us for coffee.
10. If you had worked a little harder, you would have passed your examinations sooner.

EXERCISE 84. Intermediate

Note: **The Unreal Past.**

The 2nd and 3rd types of conditional sentences (see notes to Exercise 78) require *past* and *past perfect* tenses respectively. These are really subjunctives (a form used for imagined or wished-for situations), but only the verb "to be" retains a distinctive form in modern English. (If I *were*, etc.)

The **Past Tense** form is used for a supposition or wish that takes place *now*; the **Past Perfect** for a supposition or wish that is *wholly in the past*.

Examples: I wish you weren't present at these meetings.
           (You always *are* present.)
           I wish you hadn't been present at yesterday's meeting.
           (You *were* present then.)

Here are some other expressions that use the past tenses in this way:

I wish; if only; would to God! (literary); as if; suppose! (supposing!); it's (high *or* about) time; I'd rather.

The first three are wishes that can refer to the future; they are then followed by *would*.

I wish I were sitting quietly at home. (=to be sitting there now)
I wish you would go home. (Begin now to go.)

(*In the following exercise there are no sentences with "would".*)

Put the verbs into the correct tenses:

1. I wish I (know) his name.
2. It's time we all (go) home.
3. I'd rather you (go) now.
4. It's about time you (get) the tea ready.
5. Don't you wish you (come) earlier?
6. Suppose I (get) there late!

No. 6

7. He acts as if he (know) English perfectly.
8. If only he (not eat) so much garlic!

9. If only he (not eat) so much garlic last night!
10. I'd rather you (pay) me now. Suppose he (ask) me for the money tomorrow!
11. If only he (tell) you the whole story!
12. It's high time you (have) a haircut!
13. I feel as if my head (be) on fire.
14. He said he wished he (never see) me.
15. You look as if you (can) do with a drink.
16. I'd rather you (give) me a new one instead of having it repaired as you did.
17. If only I (know) earlier, I'd have sent you a telegram.
18. I wish I (not break) it.
19. He came in, looking as if he (see) a ghost.
20. Isn't it about time you (begin) to do some work?

Section 12

QUESTION-TAGS

EXERCISE 85. Elementary and Intermediate

Note: (See also Exercise 41.) In most languages a fixed form is used for this device. In English it must vary according to the verb in the sentence that requires it. There are three simple rules:

1. Affirmative statement, negative tag; negative statement, affirmative tag.
2. Helping verbs (special finites) are repeated in the tag.
3. Other verbs have *do, does* or *did* in the tag.

Examples:
(a) He is here, isn't he? (He isn't here, is he?)
(b) You will come, won't you? (You won't come, will you?)
(c) He came yesterday, didn't he? (He didn't come yesterday, did he?)

Read the following statements and add the question-tag:

1. He is early this morning.
2. We must go now.
3. You can swim well.
4. I was very quick.

5. It could be done.
6. You won't be late.
7. This winter hasn't been cold.
8. They ought not to be here.
9. You shouldn't smoke.
10. He has finished.
11. I am not so fat as you.
12. They always work hard.
13. He speaks English well.
14. You can help him.
15. You teach English.
16. They are learning English.
17. He has a lot of books.
18. She is too young.
19. You eat very quickly.
20. We must answer the letter.
21. He is greedy.
22. George has just left.
23. He lives at the end of the road.
24. He didn't come.
25. You were there.
26. I mustn't be late.
27. Boys don't like to wash.
28. She doesn't play tennis.
29. We got home very late.
30. She sang well.

EXERCISE 86. Intermediate

Note: Special forms of Question-tag.

I am usually has the tag **aren't I?** (In literary English we sometimes find **am I not?**)

Need and **dare** do not often occur in the affirmative with a question-tag. When they do, they behave as Full Verbs.

We need to ask first, *don't we*? (Cf. We needn't ask first, *need we?*)

Used to normally takes *did* in spoken English.

They used to play together, *didn't they*? (Lit: *used they not?*)

Imperatives. These use *shall/will* for tags. A tag is very commonly used to soften a command.

Write to me, *will you*?   (rising intonation on tag)

Write to me, *won't you*?   (falling intonation on tag)

The first person imperative is the short form **Let's**, and it must not be confused with the second person of **Let** followed by **us,** which is always in the full form.

Let's do it by ourselves, *shall we*? (1st person imperative)

Let us do it by ourselves, *will you*? (2nd person; *allow us to . . .*) (This is the plural form of "Let me do it by myself, will you?")

Notice also: You'd better go, *hadn't you*?

You'd rather stay, *wouldn't you*?

Correct stress and intonation is also important for a sound understanding of these devices; there is no room to discuss this in detail here, but many exercises can be found in *Living English Speech* (*Longmans*).

Read the following statements and add the question-tag:

1. You broke the window.
2. They didn't see you.
3. That boy ran very fast.
4. You don't like sugar.
5. He can do that for you.
6. I am very stupid.
7. I am not stupid.
8. She doesn't want to go.
9. He loves fishing.
10. We ought not to have listened.
11. They should have been able to do it.
12. You knew that before.
13. He plays the violin badly.
14. They went out just now.
15. You'll have some more tea.
16. You have your lunch at one o'clock.
17. You don't have to go just yet.
18. You had a swim yesterday.
19. You needn't stay long.
20. He used to live here.
21. I am older than you.
22. You will come.
23. You would like to come.
24. I shan't be in your way.
25. I ought to ring him up.
26. He'll fall down.
27. You never used to wear a hat.
28. I'm afraid I'm a little late.
29. He hadn't met you before.
30. He made you do it again.
31. They arrived yesterday.
32. You have heard about that.
33. You like coffee.
34. You'd rather I didn't say anything.
35. He won't fall down.
36. You will come.
37. I am very late.
38. She came very late.
39. He has your book.
40. He has his breakfast at nine o'clock.
41. He has got to go now.
42. Come and see me to-morrow.
43. Let's pretend we're not here.
44. Let me have a look.
45. I'd better go.

Section 13

MISCELLANEOUS PATTERNS

EXERCISE 87. Elementary and Intermediate

Note: In spoken English the simple present and past tenses of *to have* are normally followed by *got*.

I've got a book like that at home.
He said **he'd got** one like it, too.
(*The past tense form is found mostly in Reported Speech*.)

This use of *got* is also common with *have to* (= must).
The obligation is emphasized by stressing *got*. The past tense form is found mostly in this stressed form or in Reported Speech. *Haven't got to = needn't.*

I've got to practise the piano every day.
He said *he'd go to* practice every day.
You hadn't *got* to do what *he* said. (emphatic)

Other uses of the verb "have" are not found with "got".

Say the following sentences, using a form with "got" instead of the simple verb "have".

1. I have some more at home.
2. He hadn't any like this. (*Amer.* didn't have)
3. Have you a dog?
4. I'm afraid I haven't time to do it. (*Am.* don't h.)
5. Have you the tickets?
6. He has plenty in his shop.
7. She has some lovely flowers in her garden.
8. Have they your address?
9. We have some new photos to show you.
10. The cat hasn't anything to eat. (*Am.* doesn't h.)
11. Have you someone to help you?
12. It has a bit broken off the top.
13. I've plenty of time now.
14. Have you everything you want?

15. I hadn't any money on me yesterday. (*Am.* didn't h.)
16. I haven't any now. (*Am.* don't h.)
17. He asked me for some chocolate, but I hadn't any. (*Am.* didn't h.)
18. I've enough money to buy two.
19. Has he a job now?
20. What have you to show me?
21. Haven't they anything better to do? (*Am.* don't they h.)
22. I don't have to get up so early every morning.
23. He told me he didn't have to work any more.
24. Why have you to give him so much money?
25. I'm afraid I have to go now.
26. You seem to have plenty to do.
27. Do they *have* to travel with us? (emphatic)
28. I don't have to sleep there, do I?
29. Did you know she hadn't anything to wear? (*Am.* didn't h.)
30. You don't have to do what your sister tells you.

EXERCISE 88. Elementary and Intermediate

Note: **Predicative "so" and "not".** A few verbs, the commonest being *think, suppose, believe, expect, hope, to be afraid* (*that*), are followed by "so" in place of a predicative already mentioned.

"I wonder if we shall win a prize." "*Oh, I hope so.*"
"We'll have to wait at least an hour." "*I'm afraid so.*"

"So" is also used in the negative forms of the first four.

"Does John know you are here?" "*No, I don't think so.*"
"Has he left yet?"   "*I don't believe so.*"

The other two are followed by "not" in the negative.
"I think it's going to rain." "*I hope not.*"
"Can you lend me a pound?" "*I'm afraid not.*"

(The verbs *think* and *believe* can also be followed by "not", but this makes them into *emphatic* negatives.)

Read the following sentences to the students; they are to respond with the suggested verb and "so" or "not":

1. Is there time for another cup of tea? (think)
2. He left a week ago, didn't he? (believe)

3. Your mother won't be angry with you, will she? (not suppose)
4. I expect we shall have a good time at the party. (hope)
5. It seems that the train is very late. (afraid)
6. I'm sure you'll soon get better. (hope)
7. Perhaps he will refuse to pay me. (not think)
8. We may arrive too late. (hope)
9. Wasn't Nelson a famous admiral? (think)
10. You had a very unpleasant time, I'm told. (afraid)
11. Athens is on the coast, isn't it? (believe)
12. I think it will rain tomorrow. (afraid)
13. You are having a holiday this year, aren't you? (suppose)
14. I expect this case is too heavy for you. (not think)
15. It's time to go, isn't it? (believe)
16. You haven't used this before, have you? (not think)
17. Do you think it will keep fine today? (afraid)
18. Is this book a good one? (believe)
19. Were you very late? (afraid)
20. Grammatical exercises are very dull, aren't they? (think)

EXERCISE 89. Elementary and Intermediate

Note: **Else.** This useful word is closely tied to certain pronouns; in particular the compounds of *some*, *any*, and *no* to convey the meaning "some other person" *etc.* Interrogative pronouns can also combine with *else* (but not *which?* And *Why else? When else?* are rare.

The possessive forms are **someone else's,** *etc.* The usual interrogative possessive is **Who else's?** (sometimes **Whose else?**)

Say the following sentences in a better way, using "else":

1. Have you **any other thing** to say?
2. You must see **another person.**
3. May I stay **at some other place?**
4. What **other thing** must I do?
5. I have **some other thing** to show you.
6. **What other place** can I go to?
7. **What other person** is coming with you?
8. **In what other way** can I do it?

9. Ask **some other person** to lend it to you.
10. **All the other people have** a green ticket.
11. "Haven't I seen you **in some other place**?"
12. "No, you haven't seen me **in any other place**."
13. **What other person** did you speak to?
14. **No other person** had a dog like mine.
15. What **other thing** could I do?
16. Has he **some other thing** to tell us?
17. **All the other people have** gone.
18. **What other person** did you see?
19. **At what other place** can I find one?
20. "**What other person** is coming?" "**No other person.**"
21. Have you decided on **any other thing** yet?
22. I think this is **some other person's** hat.

No. 22

23. **At what other time** could we meet?
24. If you can't find my umbrella, **any other person's** will do.
25. **In what other way** can you possibly do it.
26. **No other person's** room has been paid for.
27. I wonder if **any other person's** signature would **do** instead?
28. I wonder **what other person's** would do instead?
29. You must have mistaken me for **some other person.**
    I've never lived **in any other place** but here.
30. Isn't there **any other person's** time you can waste instead of mine?

EXERCISE 90.   Elementary and Intermediate

Note: **Comparisons.**

"He is *less stupid than* I thought" is better expressed
as "He is **not so stupid as** I thought" or
"He is **cleverer than** I thought."

Express the following sentences in the two ways suggested above.
(Most of the sentences below are not good ones in the form printed.)

1. Your house is less near than I thought.
2. This book is less big than yours.
3. This exercise is less good than your last one.
4. My mother is less old than you think she is.
5. These grapes are less expensive than those.
6. A donkey is less beautiful than a horse.
7. We're less bad than you think we are.
8. This hill is less low than I thought it was.
9. I am less light than you.
10. The grass is less short here than in our garden.
11. Apples are less cheap than oranges.
12. A tram is less quick than a bus.
13. My brother is less hard-working than me.
14. Our house is less low than yours.
15. This street is less wide than the next one.
16. My bag is less heavy than my friend's.
17. The sea was less smooth than I had hoped.
18. The river is less deep near the ford.
19. She is less proud than her sister.
20. John is much less intelligent than his sister.

EXERCISE 91.   Elementary and Intermediate

Note: **Pre-verb Adverbs.** Certain important adverbs are placed
just before the main verb of a sentence (but after the verb *to be*)

I *often see* him. I *can often see* him.
He *is often* here.

Many of these adverbs answer the question **How often?**
(*Adverbs of Frequency.*)
Often, never, sometimes, always, seldom, generally, hardly
ever, *etc.*

Other common adverbs in this position are:
almost, nearly, quite, hardly, scarcely.

He almost fell, I can't quite see the board.

These adverbs are placed in front of the Helping Verbs:

(a) For emphasis.

I never *could* understand mathematics.

He's late again! He always *is* late nowadays.

(b) When the Helping Verb stands alone.

"Can we buy stamps there?"

"We usually can." "We never can."

Read the following sentences with the given adverb:

1. I go to the pictures (often).
2. I have seen an elephant (never).
3. She is a good student (always).
4. I do my homework (usually).
5. I forget my homework (sometimes).
6. We try to work well (always).
7. We are very busy (generally).
8. The trams are full in this town (usually).
9. They have heard of it (never).
10. The student on my left (right) makes mistakes (always).
11. The student on my right (left) answers correctly (never).
12. My friend stays long (never).
13. I am going for a walk (just).
14. She has come in (just).
15. I travel by train (usually).
16. Mary can swim now (nearly).
17. She knows what to say about it (scarcely).
18. I can't understand (quite).
19. The porter was able to carry my luggage (hardly).
20. We have finished this exercise (almost).
21. I drink my tea with milk (generally).
22. He gets up before half-past nine (never).
23. He isn't late (generally), but he *was* last night (nearly).
24. "You are to do as your father tells you (always)."
    "I do (always)."
25. "I have seen a worse homework (rarely)."
    "I have (never)."

EXERCISE 92.   Elementary and Intermediate

Note: **The Infinitive.** An infinitive phrase is shorter and easier to use than a clause and is therefore preferable to a clause where there is a choice.

When the Main Clause and a Dependent Clause have the same subject, it is often possible to express the latter more concisely as an infinitive.

   Examples:
I was glad *when I heard* of your success.
I was glad *to hear* of your success.
I was sorry *when I saw* him so ill.
I was sorry *to see* him so ill.
But: *I* was glad when *he* told me of your success.
      I was sorry that *you* weren't there.
(These cannot have the shorter infinitive phrase because there are two different subjects.)

Occasionally we prefer to keep two clauses, especially if otherwise we have to use the clumsy infinitive of a defective verb:

   I was sorry (that) I couldn't come.
   (*I was sorry not to be able to come.*)

Another common use of an infinitive phrase is to replace the idea of a defining relative clause after a superlative:

   He was *the last* person *who saw* him (or ... that saw him).
   He was *the last* person *to see* him.
   (*For Defining Relatives, see Exercise* 107, *etc.*)

Object and Infinitive. There are a few important verbs that can take either an infinitive phrase (with the subject linked to the infinitive), or can have an object before the infinitive (when the object becomes the subject of the infinitive).

   Examples:
   I want **to go** home.   (*"I" is subject of* "go".)
   I want **you to go** home.   (*"You" is subject of* "go".)
   They meant **to leave** at once.
   They meant **us to leave** at once.

The most important verbs having these two patterns are: *ask, expect, intend, like, mean, prefer, (not) trouble, want.*

Replace the clauses **in heavy type** *with infinitive phrases:*

1. I was sorry **when I heard** you were ill.
2. He hopes **that he will know** soon.
3. We are happy **that we help** you.
4. You would be foolish **if you believed** all he says.
5. We should be sorry **if we left** before the end.
6. The boys did not expect **that they would pass** their examination so soon.
7. John was told **that he must not be** late.
8. The other boys only laughed **when they saw** him fall down.
9. She asked **if she might leave** the room.
10. I hope **that I shall see** you here again next week.
11. It is certain **that it will rain** if you forget your umbrella.
12. They were delighted **when they heard** of our safe arrival.
13. Don't forget you have promised **that you will come** again soon.
14. The first person **who arrived** was our own teacher.
15. We were pleased **when we learned** that you were coming, too.

Make sentences freely on the following patterns:

He asked to look at ...
He asked us to look at ...
He expects to ...
He expects his friends to ...
We meant to take ...
We meant you to ...
You needn't trouble to put ...
I must trouble you to put ...
He intended to ...
He intended you to ...

EXERCISE 93. Elementary and Intermediate

Note: **Too** (with infinitive). This adverb of excess combines with the infinitive to make a kind of negative. If the infinitive has its own subject, it is introduced by the preposition "for".

Examples:

This soup is very hot; **I can't** drink it.

This soup is **too** hot (*for me*) **to drink.**

That picture is very high; **you can't** reach it.

That picture is **too** high (*for you*) **to reach.**

Use "too" and the infinitive to express the following ideas:

1. It's very cold; we can't go out.
2. This book is very difficult; I can't read it.
3. She came very late; she couldn't hear his lecture.
4. This hat is very big; you can't wear it.
5. It's very far; we can't walk.
6. He's very stupid; he can't understand.
7. It's very big; it won't go into my pocket.
8. This mountain is very high; we can't climb it.
9. The news is very good; it can't be true.
10. It's very dark; the children can't find the way.
11. This shirt is very old; I can't wear it any more.
12. It is very wet; you mustn't go out.
13. The music is very soft; those at the back can't hear.
14. This plate is very hot; I can't touch it.
15. This grammar is very difficult; a young child can't understand it.

EXERCISE 94. Elementary and Intermediate

Note: **Enough** (with infinitive). Unlike "too", "enough" always has an affirmative meaning. It combines with an infinitive in the same way (see previous exercise). "Enough" comes *after* an adjective, but stands *before* a noun.

Examples:

He is very tall; he **can touch** the ceiling.

He is **tall enough to touch** the ceiling.

There is plenty of chalk; you **can write** on the board.

There is **enough chalk** (*for you*) **to write** on the board.

Use "enough" and the infinitive to express the following ideas:

1. You're quite clever; you can do it by yourself.
2. You're quite old now; you can have a watch.

3. I'm very tired; I can sleep all night.
4. Are you very tall? Can you reach that picture?
5. The apples are ripe; we can pick them.
6. This story is very short; the pupils can read it in one lesson.
7. The moon is very bright; I can read by it.
8. The wind is very strong; it will blow the roof off.
9. I have some money; I can pay the bill.
10. This book is very small; you can put it into your pocket.
11. My friend is very strong; he can lift you with one hand.
12. There's plenty of time; we can have another cup of coffee.
13. He plays very well; he can be a member of the team.
14. This carpet is quite big; it will cover the whole floor.
15. It's quite cold; we will wear gloves.

EXERCISE 95. Intermediate

Note: **Too/enough (with infinitive).**

Too with infinitive has a negative meaning:
It was too cold (for us) to go out.
(It was so cold that we could **not** go out.)

Enough with infinitive has an affirmative meaning:
It was cold enough to freeze our fingers.
(It was so cold that our fingers froze.)

Use either "too" or "enough" and the infinitive to express the following ideas:

1. This coffee is very hot; I can't drink it.
2. John is very tall; he can touch the ceiling.
3. This room is small; we can't all get in.
4. The weather was hot; we couldn't go out.
5. Our teacher is clever; he can tell you the answer.
6. I'm very excited; I can't think.
7. The problem is difficult; we can't explain it.
8. You are quite old; you ought to know better.
9. That orange was very sour; I couldn't eat it.
10. He was very angry; he couldn't speak to me.
11. The windows were very dirty; they couldn't see through them.

12. I think you are very strong; you can lift this box.
13. The river was very deep; they couldn't walk across.
14. He is quite well; he can go out again.
15. Our cat is very lazy; he doesn't catch mice.

Section 14

GERUND AND INFINITIVE

EXERCISE 96. Elementary and Intermediate

Note: **The Gerund** ("ing"-form).

The part of the verb ending in "-ing" is sometimes the **Present Participle** and can have the force of an adjective as well as that of a verb.

There it is, lying on the floor!
The old man, rising to his feet, began to speak.

It is sometimes a **Gerund,** and has the force of a noun as well as that of a verb.

Reading is pleasant.
Reading books is pleasant.

A number of verbs can be followed by the "-ing" form of a verb instead of the infinitive or a clause. When this is a **Gerund,** it can be the object of the main verb, and (as it is also a verb itself) can have its own object.

Examples: I don't like / letters.
I don't like / writing.
I don't like / writing letters.

Complete the following sentences with the "-ing"-form of the given verbs:

1. I began (*learn*) French when I was a little boy.
2. We don't like (*be*) late for school.
3. Don't start (*write*) until I tell you to.
4. Did you enjoy (*go*) to town and (*buy*) all these new things?
5. Do you remember (*write*) to him?
6. Don't stop (*talk*)! I like (*listen*) to you.
7. I love (*get*) letters, but I dislike (*write*) the answers.

8. I can't help (*think*) that you will miss (*come*) to see us.
9. My uncle has given up (*smoke*) and now he prefers (**eat**) sweets.
10. They have suggested (*have*) the lesson a little later. Do you mind (*come*) a little later, too?
11. I hate (*wait*) in the rain.

No. 11

12. You must practise (*read*) English aloud.
13. He went on (*look for*) the missing books long after the others had stopped (*try*) to find them.
14. I'm fond of (*read*) novels but I don't like (*see*) them as films.
15. Would you mind (*open*) the window and (*let*) a little air in?

EXERCISE 97. Elementary and Intermediate

Note: "Subject" of "-ing"-form.

Since the Gerund is a noun, it can be preceded by a possessive adjective (my, your *etc.*) or a noun in the possessive case.
This acts as its subject.

Do you mind coming early?
Do you mind *my* coming early?   (= *If I come early.*)

The possessive form is not possible with more complicated "subjects" of a gerund, and of course cannot be used for *things*. (In practice we find it used only for pronouns and proper names.) In all other cases we must use the objective (common) case.

Do you remember *me and my mother* coming to see you?

There was no sign of *the dinner* appearing before I left.
He couldn't agree to *rich and poor* being treated alike.

Because we find the objective case so frequently used in this way, it is also logical that it should occur quite commonly where a possessive case *is* possible; *i.e.* where we have a pronoun or proper name as the subject of a gerund.

Do you mind *their/them* coming too?
I don't like *his/him* coming late every time.
We didn't fancy *Mary's/Mary* living there all alone.

Some grammarians suggest that it is better style to use the possessive in the above sentences, but there is clearly no logical reason for such a preference. In literary style we certainly find the possessive used for pronouns more than the objective, but both forms are found on other occasions. (An interesting passage for a student to read is the description of David's wedding to Dora in Chapter 43 of Dickens's *David Copperfield*.)

The next two exercises ensure that the student is able to use both forms with equal ease.

Read the following, replacing the possessives in bold type by pronouns:

1. Would you mind **my** coming too?
2. I can't understand **his** behaving like that.
3. I won't have **your** coming home late every night.
4. Did you do it without **his** asking you?
5. Mother hates **our** eating things between meals.
6. I remember **their** telling us the way to their house.
7. I don't fancy **his** living with us for six months.
8. Father agreed to **my** becoming an engine-driver.
9. I really can't imagine **their** doing that.
10. Doesn't you teacher dislike **your** writing your homework in pencil?
11. The doctor doesn't mind **my** eating a little meat occasionally.
12. My parents object to **my** going out alone.
13. I don't like **their** interfering in my business.
14. I hope the weather doesn't stop **our** having a good time.
15. Do you remember **my** writing to you about it?

EXERCISE 98. Elementary and Intermediate

Note: **Subject of Gerund** (as possessive case): see notes to previous exercise.

Read the following, replacing the pronouns in bold type by possessives:

1. I don't like **you** going out alone at night.
2. I dread **him** coming back when I'm alone.
3. Please excuse **us** calling you by your first name.
4. It's no use **you** pretending to be deaf.
5. I'm afraid of **him** getting into difficulties.
6. She insisted on **me** going to lie down.
7. Their father doesn't mind **them** going away for a holiday.
8. I don't remember **you** doing that before.
9. Can you imagine **me** swimming the Channel?

No. 9

10. What does he think of **you** taking this new job?
11. I can't help **him** misunderstanding me.
12. Would you object to **me** turning on the wireless?
13. I certainly don't remember **them** making all **that noise.**
14. I don't like **you** working so hard.
15. I can't stand **you** being treated like that!

EXERCISE 99. Intermediate and Advanced

Note: More advanced gerunds ("-ing" form).

List I. Common verbs that take the gerund:

avoid	*go on* (= to continue)
consider	*keep* (*on*)
delay	*leave off* (= cease)
detest	*mention*
dislike	*mind*
escape	*miss*
enjoy	*pardon*
excuse	*put off* (=postpone)
fancy (negatives and questions)	*stop*
finish	*understand*
forgive	*appreciate*

> *can't resist*
> *can't stand*
> *can't help*
> *deny*
> *postpone*
> *risk*

Most of these can have a gerund with its subject in either objective or possessive case (*see Exercises* 97 *and* 98). The last three can have only the *possessive* case with pronouns, but the effect is very heavy; a clause (as for the third example) is preferable.

Examples:
We mustn't risk (their) being late for the concert.
The prisoner denied having seen anyone at the house.
I couldn't deny his having told the story well.
(... deny that he had told ...).
They went on walking for hours.
I recollect (your/you) telling him about it.
I can't help (their/them) not liking you.
I quite understand your/you wanting to leave.
Did he mention John's/John going to see him?
I've put off (delayed) telling you the whole truth till now.
I couldn't resist tasting it before it was cooked.
Avoid eating food that is too rich.
We escaped being asked to the meeting.

You mustn't miss seeing this exhibition.

We considered selling the old cupboards and buying book-shelves.

Please excuse (forgive, pardon) my disturbing you.

(*or:* Please excuse *etc.* me **for** disturbing you.)

List II. **Common verbs that can take either gerund or infinitive:**

advise	*like*
agree	*love*
allow	*mean*
can't bear	*permit*
begin	*prefer*
cease	*propose*
continue	*regret*
dread	*remember*
forget	*start*
hate	*study*
intend	*try*
learn	

There is sometimes a difference of meaning between the **two** constructions used with these verbs (see note to Exercise **101**).

List III. **Gerunds with meaning of Passive Infinitive.**

(Subject of verb is the *notional object* of the gerund.)

E.g.: *Your shoes* need cleaning. (= *It is necessary that someone cleans the subject of "need".*)

> *deserve*
> *merit* (not very common)
> *need*
> *want*
> *won't/doesn't/didn't bear*
> *won't/doesn't/didn't stand.*

... and expressions like: Victory is *past hoping for.*
It's *past praying for.*
That's *worth looking into* (= **examining**).
It's an idea *worth carrying out.*

Examples: Our house wants painting.
Your remark won't stand repeating.
He didn't deserve punishing.

Note that a gerund is normal after a preposition.

They objected *to his talking* so much *without saying* anything important.

Complete the following sentences using gerunds:

Example: Do you mind (I, smoke) a pipe?
            Do you mind my (*or* me) smoking a pipe?

1. She loves (swim) in the early morning.
2. Most people prefer (ride) to (walk).
3. I don't understand (he, forget) to answer my letter.
4. Why do you keep (ask) the same question?
5. I enjoy (rest) in the afternoon.
6. Do you mind (he, see) those photos again?
7. Do you remember (I, give) you this book for your birthday?
8. He dreads (sit) for the examination because he is afraid of (fail).
9. I must insist on (he, go) early; I can't risk (he, lose) the last train.
10. Does she mind (I, open) the window?
11. Please forgive (we, be) late.
12. He can't stand (I, be) right.
13. This new plan meant (we, go) by train instead of (enjoy) a sea voyage.
14. I'll never forget (you, help) me with this problem.
15. We can't agree to (they, join) us now.
16. We shall go on (ask) them for help, even if they can no longer stand (we, come) to see them every day.
17. Do you think his idea is worth (consider)?
18. I'm sure you won't mind (I, point out) that very small children need (look after) a great deal more than older ones.
19. Please excuse (we, not come) earlier.
20. The doctor advised (go) to bed early, so I can't understand (you, want) to stay up so late.

No. 20

EXERCISE 100.   Intermediate and Advanced

Note: (See previous exercise.)

List IV.   **Objective case + "-ing"** (*present participle*):
(The verbs in this list are sometime confused with those taking the gerund; the "-ing"-form here *never* has the possessive as its subject.)

feel	*observe*
watch	*perceive* (not very common)
hear	*see*
listen to	*smell*
notice	

> *have* (not in present tense)
> *can imagine*
> *she kept him waiting, etc.*
> *she caught me taking them, etc.*
> *we'll set/start/get them working, etc.*

The first eight of these can also take the infinitive. (*See Exercise 101 for difference of meaning.*)

Examples: We heard them coming.
I can smell the fish cooking.
We noticed her crying.
He'll have us speaking English in three months.

Complete the following sentences by using the "-ing"-form of the given verbs:

1. They liked (see) (we, play) together.
2. Did you notice (he, read) my letter?
3. I observed (they, watch) (John, play) the piano.
4. I can't imagine (he, agree) with you.
5. Can you smell (something, burn)?
6. I always enjoy (watch) (he, act) Shakespeare.
7. After lunch he'll set (we, work) on the problem.
8. Have I kept (you, wait) long?
9. We could feel the rain (beat) against our faces.
10. I can't imagine (he, pay) the money without (you, ask) him.[1]

---

[1] N.B. The last part of this sentence, controlled by the preposition *without*, is a gerund, not a present participle.

11. Haven't you noticed (they, watch) (we, eat) our dinner?
12. I saw (you, go) to school yesterday.
13. I can hear (they, come) downstairs.
14. He saw (they, play) near his garden and later caught (they, steal) his apples.
15. We listened to (he, read) poetry.

EXERCISE 101. Intermediate and Advanced

Note: **Infinitive compared with "-ing"-form.**

Eight verbs of List IV in the previous exercise can take the infinitive instead of the present participle. The *infinitive* describes a complete action; the *present participle* describes the action in progress (like a Continuous Tense form):

I saw him *walking* across the road. (= *on the way across.*)
I saw him *walk* across the road. (= *from one side to the other.*)

The verbs of List II in Exercise 99 may take the infinitive instead of the gerund. The general difference is that the infinitive is more usual when we are talking about one single occasion:

I prefer walking to riding. (*In general.*)
"Let's take a bus." "No, I prefer to walk." (*On this occasion.*)

I like looking at your photos. (*In general.*)
I should like to look at your photos. (*Now.*)

(Note this use of *should/would* with **love/like/hate** to describe the Real Present or near future).

Remember and **forget** are both used in two different senses. They describe:
  (*a*) the mechanism of memory (*taking infinitive with "to"*),
  (*b*) (not) to have recollection or memory of something (*taking the gerund*).

  Examples:

I must remember to pay you for the tickets. (= *must not forget.*)
I don't remember paying you for the tickets. (= *can't recall, bring to mind.*)

I forgot to collect your homework yesterday. (= *didn't remember.*)
I shall never forget going with you to see the President. (= *will always have this memory.*)

Mean (= *intend*) takes infinitive with " to ".

(It) **means** (= *signifies*) is a 3rd-person form that is followed by a gerund.

I meant to come early today.

A party tonight will mean (our) working extra hard tomorrow.

Lack of transport meant (our) having to walk over the mountain.

A few expressions use *for* with the gerund when looking back to the past, and *to* with the infinitive for present or future.

Examples:

I paid him for mending my radio. (= paid *after* mending.)

I paid him to mend my radio. (= paid *before* mending.)

He was kept indoors for being naughty.

He was kept indoors to do his homework.

Notice also:

I regretted saying it was your fault. (= *was* sorry because I said ...)

I regret having said it was your fault. (= *am* sorry because I said ...)

I regret to say it was your fault. (= am sorry that I must now say ...)

Allow and **permit,** when followed by a (pro)noun, take an *infinitive*; otherwise they take a *gerund*:

They don't allow (permit) us to cycle in the park.

They don't allow (permit) cycling in the park.

The verb **try** with an infinitive means "to make an effort or an attempt", with a gerund it means "to make an experiment, to test".

He tried to speak French to us. (= *made an effort to do so.*)

He tried speaking French to us. (= *he spoke in French, hoping we should understand him better.*)

He tried to stand on his head. (= *made the attempt.*)

His feet were tired, so I told him to try standing on his head! (= *in order to get his feet off the ground.*)

Notice the phrase **to have an opportunity of** (with gerund) or **there will be an opportunity to** (with infinitive); the latter usually means "a convenient moment" and is normally introduced by some part of the verb "to be".

We may have an opportunity of going to England next year.

This will be a good opportunity (for you) to ask for more books.

The phrase **to have occasion to** is always with the infinitive; it means *to have a reason for going*:

When I next have occasion to visit England, I'll take you with me.

Put the verbs in brackets into their correct form (sometimes alternatives will be possible).

1. I must ask you (stop) (sing).
2. Let me (help) you (get) the answer right.
3. They told him (start) (look for) some work at once.
4. We have decided (allow) him (do) as he pleases.

No. 4

5. He is fond of (try) (mend) broken clocks.
6. I heard him (say) that he wanted (buy) the house.
7. Can you (manage) (finish) (pack) these parcels yourself?
8. I should love (see) you (play) tennis.
9. Our teacher promised (help) us (prepare) for the examination.
10. She hoped (arrange) (come) early (help) (cut) the bread for the party.
11. For some time we watched them (try) (catch) fish.
12. We hope (have) an opportunity of (see) him tomorrow.
13. This will be an opportunity for you (tell) him about the new play.

14. Please excuse (I, say) so, but it is very difficult (spell) English correctly.
15. We've often had occasion (complain) of (he, come) late.
16. They let us (watch) the men (chop) down the trees.
17. I hate (get up) early.
18. I saw him (help) her (cook) the dinner.
19. I hope you're not going to keep me (wait) all day.
20. Would you mind (watch) the teacher (demonstrate) so as to (learn) (swim) more quickly.
21. I forgot (remind) her that my coat button needs (sew on).
22. We must remember (start) (revise) our verbs next lesson.
23. I remember (ask) him (lend) me his new book last night.
24. I dislike (study) on a fine afternoon.
25. I should like (watch) these men (mend) the road for a few minutes.
26. I forgot (remind) you (ask) your friend (bring back) the book he borrowed.
27. May I ask you (begin) (eat) now, without (wait) for the others to come?
28. It's no use (you, pretend) (be) asleep.
29. I should love (go) to the theatre with you tonight; I hate (go out) alone.
30. If the orange is sour, try (put) some sugar on it.

Section 15

INTERROGATIVES

EXERCISE 102. Elementary

Note: **As subject.** The following forms are possible:

Who? for persons in general (*pronoun*).
   Who broke my pencil? (*of all possible people*)

What? for things in general (*pronoun*).
   What has happened? (*of all possible things*)

What? for persons or things in general (*adjective*).
What books are these?
What people live in this country?

Which? for persons or things selected from some limited **group**
(*pronoun and adjective*).
Which of you can answer my question? (*limited choice*)
Which house is yours, No. 32 or No. 34? (*limited choice*)

(*Very often it is equally sensible to use either the limited or the general form.*)

Add the correct question-word to the following questions:

1. ... went with you to London?
2. ... of these books is your favourite?
3. ... is my place?
4. ... came in just now?
5. ... will cook the dinner today?
6. ... arrived first?
7. ... dress is the prettiest?
8. ... bus goes to Charing Cross?
9. ... asked you to write this?
10. ... has taken my scissors?
11. ... is wrong with the clock?
12. ... left the light on?
13. ... is your friend's name?
14. ... is the healthier place, the country or the seaside?
15. ... is the answer?
16. ... is your grocer?
17. ... of those young men is her fiancé?
18. ... language is the easiest to learn?
19. ... gave you those flowers?
20. ... is wrong with that exercise?
21. ... is smoking here?
22. ... is the way to the station?
23. ... would like a cup of tea?
24. ... painted that picture?
25. ... is the matter?

EXERCISE 103. Elementary

Note: **As objective and possessive case.**

Who? What? and **Which?** are used for the *object* as well as the subject:

> What (letter) comes after A? (*subject*)
> What (book) *did you read* yesterday? (*object*)
>
> Which came first—the chicken or the egg? (*subject*)
> Which (poem in this book) *do you like* best? (*object*)
>
> Who saw you yesterday? (*subject*)
> Who *did you see* yesterday? (*object*)

Notice that when the interrogative is not the subject of the sentence, the usual inversion (*subject/verb*) is needed; it is printed *in italics* in the above examples. It is this feature alone that tells us whether the interrogative is subject or object.

Whom? is an alternative object for persons, but it is confined to literary styles. It need not be used in any of the interrogative exercises in this book unless a written style is being practised.

Possessive Case. Only **Whose?** (*for persons*) exists:

> Whose book is this? (Whose is this book?)
> Whose book do you want?

(For things we must use the preposition "of". See Exercise 105.)

Add the question-word to the following questions:

1. ... do you want?
2. ... book are you reading?
3. ... is going to the cinema tonight?
4. ... of these girls is the youngest?
5. ... hat is this, mine or yours?
6. ... is the matter with him?
7. ... of you can answer that question?
8. ... is John doing?
9. ... has finished the exercise?
10. ... are those people doing?
11. ... has broken the window?
12. ... are you meeting at four o'clock?
13. ... have they done?

14. ... has eaten my sandwich?
15. ... did you want to see?
16. ... are you writing?
17. ... picture do you prefer, this or that?
18. ... asked you to come?
19. ... was that noise?
20. ... is your hat? (... hat is yours?)
21. ... did I say?
22. ... opened my letter?
23. ... European language is the easiest to learn?
24. ... can I do to help?
25. ... pencil is this, Tom's or Harry's?

EXERCISE 104. Elementary and Intermediate

Note: **Interrogative as subject or object** (revision). *See Exercises 102 and 103.*

Change the following statements into questions asking about the words in **bold type**:

> *Example:* He is reading **a book**.
> **What** is he reading?

1. She is wearing **a new hat**.
2. **I** have been to the Zoo.
3. **They** are sitting under the trees.
4. **This** is my favourite melody.
5. My name is **Mrs. Buttons**.
6. **That** tooth is hurting me.
7. I want to see **you**.
8. That lady is **my friend**.
9. **Someone** has used my fountain-pen.
10. This glass is **his**.
11. **They** have just come in.
12. We saw **the king** yesterday.
13. I want **his** book.
14. **Mary** ate it.
15. I'll give you **the brown one**.
16. I bought him **a present**.

17. Cows eat **grass**.
18. **Father** has taken the newspaper.
19. The boy learned **many subjects** at school.
20. The dog bit the **little girl**.
21. **This** shop sells good cakes.
22. The doctor told her **to stay in bed**.
23. I spilled **the ink**.
24. **That** one is better.
25. That house is **mine**.

EXERCISE 105. Elementary and Intermediate

Note: **Interrogatives with prepositions.** The most natural position for the preposition is after the verb. The possessive case for *things* is made in this way with "of".

We were talking about holidays.
What were you talking *about*?

We were speaking to John just now.
Who were you speaking *to* just now?

This is a part of a table.
What's this a part *of*?

What for? Three important uses:
(a) *With nouns. What* are these sticks *for*? (= for what purpose?)
(b) *Compound verbs.* What are you *looking for*? (= to look for something.)
(c) *With other verbs. What* are you sitting here *for*? (= why?)

The preposition is put in front of the interrogative for a number of fixed phrases that might occur as questions, such as *under what circumstances? for what purpose? by what standards? by whose order?*

(In a rather heavy literary or rhetorical style we sometimes also find the preposition in front of the interrogative in places where it would more naturally come after the verb. "Whom" *must* be used when the preposition precedes it. See note on "whom" in Exercise 103. None of the interrogative sentences in this book require this style.)

At whom are you laughing? (*unnatural, heavy style*)
Who are you laughing at? (*natural style*)

E

Add **either** *the missing question-word* **or** *the missing pre-position to the following questions:*

1.   ... are you thinking about?
2.   ... was she dancing with?
3.   ... chair was I sitting on?
4.   What are they looking ...?
5.   What is she talking ...?
6.   Who is she talking ...?

No. 6

7.   ... shall I give this to?
8.   What are you listening ...?
9.   Who is she writing ... ?
10. ... street do you live in?
11. ... did Joan give my newspaper to?
12. What are they laughing ... ?
13. ... book are you looking for?
14. ... cup were you drinking out of?
15. ... did you wash it with?
16. ... room shall I sleep in?
17. What town do you come *from* ... ?
18. ... dress shall I put on?
19. Who are you waiting ... ?
20. ... school did your friend go to?
21. What is butter made ... ?
22. ... library did you get this book from?
23. What train shall we go ... ?
24. Do you know who this parcel is ... ?
25. ... are you laughing at now?

EXERCISE 106.   Intermediate

Note: **Revision of interrogatives.** Other important question-words are *where? when? why? how?* The prepositions "from" and "to" are commonly used with *where?* and are placed after the verb:

> Where have you come from?
> Where are you going (to)?

Notice also the important question-form:
> *What* is he *like?*

Ask questions about the words in **bold type.**

1. I'm looking at **him.**
2. She wants to speak to **you.**
3. My friend is waiting for **me.**
4. They are staying with **some friends.**
5. I am laughing at **a funny picture.**
6. They were drinking out of **bottles.**
7. She is writing to **her mother.**
8. He is working for **Thomas Cook and Sons.**
9. The class was reading about **Shakespeare.**
10. He is talking about **politics.**
11. I gave it to **my brother.**
12. We are going to **the Ritz** cinema.
13. She is looking for **a pin.**
14. The children were playing with **some new toys.**
15. The school-children covered their books with **brown paper.**
16. A tailor sews with **a needle.**
17. Shoes are made of **leather.**
18. That handsome man over there is **Mr. Green.**
19. I am coming back **on Friday.**
20. You left your glasses **on the table.**
21. I have **two** cigarettes.
22. Oregon is **an American state.**
23. I am going to Suez with **my parents.**
24. **Everybody** says he is a good writer.
25. She is **a very charming girl.**

Section 16

RELATIVES

EXERCISE 107. **Elementary**

Note: **General remarks.**

Relative clauses are usually introduced by the pronouns *who,* *whom, whose, which, that,* and *what*; by the adjectives *which* and *what*; or by the adverbs *when, where* and sometimes *why*.

The two main classes of relative are:

1. **Defining Relative.**
   (The relative clause is essential to the meaning because it defines the subject, telling us "which one".)

   The man gave me this book.   (*Not clear*; which man?)
   The man *who was speaking to you* gave me this book.
   The man *you saw yesterday* gave me this book.
   The man *you were speaking to* gave me this book.

2. **Non-defining Relative.**
   (The relative clause adds to our information but is not necessary; the main clause is perfectly clear without it.)

   His brother John gave me this book. (*Quite clear*.)
   His brother John, *who lives in London*, gave me this book.
   His brother John, *whom you met yesterday*, gave me his book.

   Class 1 (*defining*) is much more important than
   Class 2 because it is more commonly used.

   Defining Relative, subject and object.
Subject (*people*):	who,	(that)
Subject (*things*):	that,	(which)
Object (*people*):	that,	(whom)
Object (*things*):	that,	(which).

Objective case of Defining Relative is usually omitted altogether. The bracketed forms above are less usual; students are advised not to use them in the following exercises.

Examples:

The boy who sat next to you is my friend.
The tree that stands by the gate has lovely flowers.
The boy you saw at the party is my friend. ("that" *omitted*)
The tree we planted last year is growing well. ("that" *omitted*)

N.B.—Defining Relative clauses are never separated from the main sentence by means of commas; the whole sentence is one unit.

Add the missing relative, but where possible (i.e. in the objective case) make a contact clause (without a relative pronoun):

1. The man ... you want has just left.
2. The lady ... was here yesterday has gone to London.
3. The magazine ... you lent me is very interesting.
4. The fish ... I ate yesterday was not good.

No. 4

5. The street ... leads to the school is very wide.
6. The flowers ... I cut this morning are still fresh.
7. The dress ... you are wearing is lovely.
8. The person ... is sitting next to me is not very clever.
9. The man ... cut your hair did it very badly.
10. The letter ... we received today had no stamp on it.
11. The boy ... threw that stone will be punished.
12. The doctor ... she visited is famous.
13. The noise ... you hear is only our dog fighting.
14. The pencil ... is lying on the desk is mine.
15. The tree ... stands near the gate has lovely flowers.
16. The pen ... I lost was not a good one.
17. The pudding ... she made this morning is a very good one.
18. The flowers ... my friend gave me have died.

19. The little boy ... brings the milk hasn't been for three days.
20. The eggs ... I bought yesterday are bad.

EXERCISE 108.   Elementary

Note: **Defining Relative, possessive and prepositional.**

Possessive   (*people*):   whose
Possessive   (*things*):   of which (whose)
Prepositional (*people*):   that ... to, etc.
Prepositional (*things*):   that ... to, etc.
(The relative "that" is usually omitted.)

Examples:

This is the boy whose work I was telling you about.
The book whose (of which the) cover is torn is mine.
(*We avoid this clumsy construction when we can. E.g.* The book with (the) torn covers is mine.)
The man you were talking to is my father. ("that" *omitted*)
The book you were looking at isn't mine. ("that" *omitted*)

Although "who" is usually preferred to "that" as the relative pronoun for people in the subjective case, we usually find "that" (rarely "who") with **superlatives,** and often with **any** and **only.**

Examples:

He was one of the strongest men that ever lived.
He's the only boy that got ten marks out of ten.

Add relative pronouns where needed (that is, make a contact clause, without the relative, where this is possible):

1. The book ... I was reading yesterday was a detective story.
2. The man ... you spoke to in the street is my English teacher.
3. There's the lady ... purse has been stolen.
4. The people ... you were living with in London are coming to see you.
5. The picture ... you were talking about has been sold.
6. "People ... live in glass houses shouldn't throw stones."
7. Buy it back from the man ... you sold it to.
8. Can you remember the person ... you took it from?

9. Where is there a shop ... sells picture-postcards?
10. What's that music ... you are listening to?
11. I don't like the house ... he lives in.
12. The people ... are looking at that house are my parents.
13. The house ... they are looking at is my house.
14. And the girl ... you see at the door is my sister.
15. The knife ... we use to cut the bread with is very sharp.
16. I'm afraid that's all ... I've got.
17. The man ... is sitting at the desk is the secretary.
18. The man ... you see at the desk is the secretary.
19. The glass ... you are drinking out of hasn't been washed.
20. The man ... you are talking about left last week.

EXERCISE 109. Elementary and Intermediate

Note: **Non-defining Relative.** (See Exercise 107.)

1. The pronoun "that" is not used at all.
2. The non-defining relative clause is enclosed between commas.
3. The pronoun can never be omitted as in Exercises 107 and 108.

	People.	*Things.*
Subject:	..., who ...,	..., which ...,
Object:	..., whom ...,	..., which ...,
Possessive:	..., whose ...,	..., of which ...,
		(..., whose ...,)

Prepositional: ..., to *etc.* whom ..., ..., to *etc.* which ...,
            (..., who(m) ... to *etc.*), (..., which ... to *etc.*)

The bracketed forms are occasionally found, but students should not use them.

Examples:

My brother Bob, who met you yesterday, is coming with us.
My brother Bob, whom you met yesterday, is coming with us.
My brother Bob, whose letter I've just read to you, is coming with us.
My brother Bob, about whom we were talking, is coming with us.

Non-defining relatives are rare in the spoken language, but quite normal in written English. The ideas in the examples above would in each case be expressed as two sentences in spoken English.

For example:

My brother Bob's coming with us. You met him yesterday, didn't you?

You remember (our) talking about my brother Bob? Well, he's coming with us.

Add relative pronouns to the following sentences:

1. My sister, . . . you met yesterday, wants to speak to you.
2. Her father, . . . has been to Paris, has just returned.
3. The London train, . . . should arrive at 2.30, is late.
4. Flies, . . . come mostly in the summer, carry disease.
5. Oxford University, . . . is one of the oldest in the world, has many different colleges.
6. Swimming, . . . is a good sport, makes people strong.
7. Julius Caesar, . . . was a great general, was also a writer.
8. Grass, . . . cows and horses love, is always green in England.
9. Air, . . . we breathe, is made up of many gases.
10. Tommy and Mary, . . . are playing in the garden, are very naughty children.
11. George Washington, . . . became President of the United States, never told a lie.
12. Grammar, . . . I dislike very much, is good for me.
13. In Norway, . . . is a Baltic country, you can see the midnight sun.
14. Smoking, . . . is a bad habit, is nevertheless popular.
15. The teacher in the next class, . . . name I can never remember, makes a lot of noise.
16. He is a famous scientist, about . . . many books have been written.
17. Geometry, about . . . I know nothing, seems a very dull subject.
18. The Tower of London, about . . . a lecture is to be given tomorrow, is a famous historic building.
19. Beethoven, . . . music you have just been listening to, was one of the world's finest composers.
20. Chess, . . . is a very old game, is difficult to play.

EXERCISE 110. Intermediate

Note: **Revision of Relative Clauses.** (See last three exercises.)

The words **much, the little, the few,** are regularly followed by *that*, not *who* or *which*.

The little that was left was very good.
The little (that) you gave me was very good.
The few that waited managed to get some tickets.

Double relatives. When two relative clauses follow one another, the second is usually in the "wh–" form. It does not matter if it is co-ordinate with the first relative (joined with *and* or *but*), or further defines the subject.

Examples: This is the paper I read every day and which I find so interesting.
You are the only person I've ever met who could do it.
Words between brackets are forms that are occasionally found but which should not be taught.

Combine the following pairs of sentences by means of relative clauses:

1. **The Irawaddy** flows through many large swamps. **It** is one of the most important rivers in Asia.
2. We must certainly see **the antiquities** of Egypt. Such a great deal has been written about **them**.
3. **The great fire** of London destroyed a large part of the city. **It** broke out in 1666.
4. **Mr. Jones** came here only last week. **He** is living next door to us.
5. This is **the man**. I gave the money to **him** yesterday.
6. **My aunt** is very kind to me. I am living with **her**.
7. Is that **the new station**? You pointed **it** out to me last week.
8. Bring me **the cigarettes**. I left **them** on the **table**. **The table** stands by the window.
9. **My teacher** says that I ought to pass my examination. I have great confidence in **him**.
10. **The matter** has been settled. You were talking about **it** last night.

11. I've seen only **a few**. **They** were all black. (Begin with "The few ...".)
12. **The best play** is probably *King Lear*. Shakespeare wrote it but I haven't read it.
13. Last week I went to see **the town**. He used to live in **that town**.
14. He could let me have only **one pound** of tea. I must give a quarter of **it** to my sister.
15. This is **the horse**. **It** kicked **the policeman**. I saw **him** trying to clear away **the crowd**. **The crowd** had collected to watch **a fight**. Two men had started **the fight**.

EXERCISE 111.   Elementary and Intermediate

Note: **Relative and Interrogative links.**

The words practised in the last few exercises, *who*, *which*, *what*, *where*, *when etc.*, help to make a very common type of complex sentence. The simplest type uses an infinitive phrase (see also Exercise 92).

The infinitive is used when the subject is the same for both sections; the time is always future.

I don't know which to take.   (= which I ought to take)
Cf. *I don't know which I took.*

"Who" is usual for both subjective and objective cases, except in very formal or literary style, where "whom" is sometimes found in the objective case.

Add the missing joining-word:

1. I don't know ... to do.
2. He has forgotten ... to go.
3. I have no idea ... to ask.
4. Do you know ... to make coffee?
5. Ask him ... to put it.
6. I don't understand ... to drive a car.
7. You must go ... he tells you.
8. Can you suggest ... to write?
9. She doesn't know ... dress to wear.
10. I can't remember ... to do it.

11. We don't know ... to show it to.
12. I shan't forget ... to find it again.
13. He doesn't know ... to open it with.
14. My friend couldn't remember ... way to go.
15. They don't know ... your house is.
16. I can't imagine ... you are so cross with me.

No. 16

17. She doesn't understand ... to do the exercise.
18. I can't think ... to buy for dinner.
19. Have you decided ... to ask to the party?
20. They don't know ... to meet us tomorrow.

EXERCISE 112. Intermediate

Note: **Relative and Interrogative links.**

Some verbs can be followed by an object that is itself the subject of the infinitive.

Compare: *He* asked to leave the room.
             He asked *us* to leave the room.

The commonest verbs of this second type are:

  advise, instruct, persuade, teach, tell, warn.

Add the missing joining-word:
1. They told us ... to write to.
2. I advised them ... to go.
3. He told me ... book to take.
4. They instructed us ... to behave.
5. He taught us ... to catch fish.

O

6. We persuaded them ... to do.
7. He warned us ... to avoid.
8. We'll teach him ... to say.
9. We can advise you ... to consult.
10. He warned them ... not to eat.

EXERCISE 113.   Elementary and Intermediate

Note: **Relative and Interrogative links.**

When the subject of each section is different we must use a clause instead of the infinitive.

> *Examples: We* don't know who *she* was speaking to.
> *He* asked me how *they* had done it.

Add the missing joining-word:

1. I wonder ... he means.
2. I have no idea ... he arrived.
3. Do you know ... you are talking to?
4. I have no idea ... he will come.
5. Will you please tell me ... soon you can finish it?
6. I wonder ... hat this is, it's certainly not mine.
7. You haven't told me ... you did last night.
8. Lots of people don't know ... Vladikavkaz is.
9. Can you tell us ... road leads to the station?
10. I've forgotten ... she gave it to.
11. I wonder ... she married.
12. I can't think ... she married him.
13. Have they told you ... time to come?
14. Can you see ... is coming down the street?
15. You must tell the librarian ... book you are taking.
16. She hasn't written to tell me ... she is coming.
17. The grocer says he doesn't know ... he sent it to.
18. Have you heard ... is coming to stay with me?
19. We don't know ... she has gone.
20. Can you tell me ... this box is so heavy?
21. Do you know ... makes the sun hot?
22. Nobody knows ... you put your shoes.

23. I want to know ... told you about it.
24. Show me ... this machine works.
25. I am not sure ... their train arrives.

Section 17

"THERE IS" AND "IT IS", ETC.

EXERCISE 114.   Elementary and Intermediate

Note: **There is,** *etc.* This construction is sometimes called Preparatory "there". It is the most usual way of describing the existence of an *indefinite* subject.

There are two books on the table. [ðərə 'tu: buks ...]

There was a good film at the Odeon last week. [ðəwəzə 'gud ...]

(The forms *Two books are on the table,* and *A good film was at the Odeon,* are possible grammatically but rarely used.)

In these examples the word **there** has lost its force as an adverb of place and is pronounced in a weak form [ðə(r)]. This pronunciation is all that distinguishes it from its full meaning as an adverb of place.

There's a book on the floor. [ðəz ə 'buk ...]

There's your book, on the floor! ['ðɛəz jɔ: 'buk ...]

Add the correct form of **There is** *to the following:*

1. ... two dogs in the garden.
2. ... a lot of people in the park yesterday.
3. ... a train coming now.
4. ... (negative) another train for at least two hours.
5. ... a few changes since you left last week.
6. ... some chocolates on this plate when I went out just now.
7. ... one for you tomorrow.
8. ... plenty of knives in the drawer.
9. ... only a footpath here last year.
10. ... no mistakes in your last exercise.
11. ... no fruit on this tree for many years.
12. ... a thunderstorm soon, I think.
13. ... four hundred children in the school this year.

14.   ... an accident outside our house last night.
15.   ... a lot of visitors this morning.
16.   ... some more work for you tomorrow.
17.   ... a lot more snow since yesterday.
18.   ... (*negative*) enough time to finish it tomorrow.
19.   ... no pictures in this dictionary.
20.   ... another football match next Saturday.

EXERCISE 115.   Elementary and Intermediate

Note: **It is,** *etc.* This construction is sometimes called Preparatory "it". The two main uses are:

1. To introduce a complex subject (*phrase or clause*).
     It is wrong not to do as you're told.
     (= Not to do as you're told/is wrong.)
     It was a pity (that) they hadn't told us sooner.

2. "It" used as a meaningless subject for a number of impersonal verbs (especially weather) and other expressions of time and measurement.
         It's raining hard.
         It was foggy/frosty/snowing, *etc.*, last night.
         "It's a long way to Tipperary."
         It's half a mile from here to the school.

Add the correct form of **It is** *to the following:*

1.   ... a pity (that) she is so stupid.
2.   ... fine tomorrow, I think.
3.   ... a shame to spend all this money.
4.   ... stupid not to go yesterday.
5.   ... not very far to walk.
6.   ... a great day when he passes his examination. (Note that "a great day" is not the true subject of this sentence.)
7.   ... nice having you to tea last Wednesday.
8.   ... wonderful to see you again next week.
9.   ... possible (that) he doesn't understand English.
10.   ... strange (that) she didn't speak to you.
11.   ... very wet last month, and now ... windy.
12.   ... raining for three hours without stopping.
13.   ... a long time since I saw you.

14. ... cruel to beat a dog like that.
15. Our teacher thinks ... better to take the examination next summer.
16. ... his own fault that he missed the volley-ball match.
17. ... past four o'clock when they arrived.
18. ... my constant wish to visit Europe since I was a boy.
19. ... wrong of you not to have answered his last letter.
20. ... here that I first met him.

EXERCISE 116. Intermediate

Note: **There is**, *etc.*, and **It is**, *etc.* (See previous two exercises.)

The following types of sentence about time and place are sometimes confused.

  (a) It is a long time since ... (= *the time since ... has been long*)
  (b) It is time to go home. (= *this is the correct moment*)
  (c) There is time to go home. (= *we have time; enough time exists*)
  (a) It's a long way to school. (= *the distance is long*)
  (b) There's a long way to go yet before we arrive. (= *we still have this distance to go; this distance exists for us*)

Add the correct form of **There is** *or* **It is** *to the following:*

1. ... easy to understand why he hasn't come back.
2. ... time to go to bed.
3. ... very strange that we should both arrive together.
4. ... no one at home when I called for him.
5. ... a few sandwiches left over from yesterday.
6. ... two guests coming for the week-end.
7. ... no place like home.
8. ... hard to decide what was the best thing to do.
9. ... still several empty seats in the plane when I arrived.
10. ... time to finish this exercise before we go.
11. ... a long time since I saw such a beautiful sunset.
12. ... a light in the kitchen when I got home.
13. ... few able to understand his lecture yesterday.
14. ... no time for tea if we don't hurry.
15. ... fine today.

16. ... a good thing to be accurate.
17. ... a man standing under that tree ten minutes ago.
18. ... here that I saw him.
19. ... a post office in the village.
20. ... nothing left if we don't go soon.
21. ... a long time since I had a holiday.
22. ... often a rainbow after rain.
23. ... a pity (that) you can't come with me.
24. ... too early to leave yet.
25. ... a beautiful park near my home.
26. ... not true to say that she is my friend.
27. ... a dog running across the road.
28. ... a train which leaves at nine o'clock.
29. ... not far from my house to the station.
30. ... time to go there on foot if you want to.
31. ... not the season for bananas.
32. ... nearly time to say good night.
33. ... a game in some parts of the world called tric-trac, which English people know as backgammon.
34. ... time for your medicine in half an hour.
35. ... time for another cigarette before she gets back.

Section 18

REPORTED SPEECH

EXERCISE 117. Elementary

Note: **Imperative.** This becomes an **infinitive** in reported (indirect) speech, and is usually introduced by one of these verbs: *tell, ask, order, request.*

"*Go away!*" I told (asked) him, *etc.* to go away.
"*Don't be afraid.*" He told me not to be afraid.

The verbs **tell** and **say.** The chief uses are:

Tell. Never used to introduce the actual words spoken.
Always needs a personal (indirect) object *in reported speech*.

(*a*)   He tells *us* (that) he is a student.
(*b*)   I told *him* to go away.
(*c*)   We spent the time telling funny stories.

Say. Never followed by an infinitive (cf. (*b*) above).
More often introduces actual words spoken than reported
speech.

(*a*)   I said that I couldn't come.
(*b*)   "I can't come," I said.

Notice also the word-order:

I said "Hello" to him. / I said to him that ...
I told him the truth. / I told him that ...

*Put into Reported Speech, using any suitable pronouns with
the given verbs:*

1.   Come here!   (I asked)
2.   Copy the words into your notebooks.   (The teacher told)
3.   Don't do it again!   (Ask)
4.   Write quickly!   (Tell)
5.   Sit down!   (We asked)
6.   Pick it up!   (He ordered)
7.   Don't drop it!   (Tell!)
8.   Look out!   (I told)

No. 8

9. Open the door!   (I asked)
10. Come at five o'clock!   (He told)
11. Sing a song!   (They asked)
12. Come in!   (He ordered)
13. Clean the blackboard!   (He asked)
14. Put it on the table!   (I told)
15. Don't speak until you are spoken to!   (I told)

EXERCISE 118.   Elementary

Note: **Statements.** When the reporting verb is in the *Present,* *Present Perfect,* or *Future tense,* the report is in the same tense as the actual spoken words. We sometimes have to change the personal pronouns, of course.

> "*I am very sorry.*"
> He will tell you ⎫
> He says   ⎬ (that) he is very sorry.
> He has just told me ⎭
> The conjunction "that" is usually omitted.

Put the following sentences into the Reported Speech form:

1. We are very late.   (*He says*)
2. I want to speak to you.   (*He says*)
3. We have finished our work.   (*They say*)
4. He is ready to come with us.   (*He has told me*)
5. They do not know you.   (*I have explained*)
6. She has done her homework well.   (*The teacher will tell her*)
7. We are living in another house now.   (*They tell me*)
8. I have been shopping all the morning.   (*She says*)
9. She has written me a long letter.   (*He tells me*)
10. We have not heard the news.   (*They say*)
11. I like oranges better than bananas.   (*She has explained*)
12. He is sitting over there.   (*I've told you*)
13. You are not working hard enough.   (*Our teacher says*)
14. You have been very quick.   (*They will tell me*)
15. They are waiting outside.   (*I've told him*)

EXERCISE 119. Elementary and Intermediate

Note: **Statements.** When the reporting verb is in *past time*, the tenses of the actual spoken words are related to this past time and change accordingly. The usual changes are:

> *he goes* to *he went*
> *he will go* to *he would go*
> *he has gone* and *he went* to *he had gone*
> *he would go* to *he would have gone*

> Pronouns may have to change according to the sense of the report (as in the previous exercise).
> It is also sometimes logically necessary to change certain adverbs of place and time into more "distant" ones to suit past time.

"I am *here* to help you."	He *said* he was *there* to help them.
"*This* isn't mine."	He *said that* wasn't his.
"I saw him *yesterday*."	He *said* he had seen him *the day before*.
"I'll come *next week*."	He *said* he would come *the week after*.

> ... (also the *previous day* or *the following week*)

But these changes are not *always* necessary. For example, if *next week* is still in fact *next week* because the report dates back only a few hours into the past, then we will not change it.

He told me (*just now*) that he would come again next week.

Put the following sentences into Reported Speech; introduce them with **said** *or* **told** *or any other suitable past tense:*

1. I am ill.
2. I met him last year.
3. They will be here soon.
4. She has finished now.
5. I am living in London.
6. I've just been to the butcher's.

No. 6

7. I can come next week.
8. I don't know what he'll say.
9. Wait till I come.
10. I think she is married.
11. I fell downstairs.
12. I'll leave it on the table.
13. I'm sorry I'm late.
14. I am very stupid.
15. She is quite charming but hasn't much sense.
16. He can come in when I have finished my work.
17. The clock will never work again if you try to mend it.
18. I'll come as soon as I can.
19. I was very ill yesterday.
20. I have never been here before.
21. I haven't done my homework.
22. You may have to stay in bed for a week.
23. She will be here in half an hour if she isn't late.
24. That is the last time I saw him.
25. I shall try to be in time today. I'm sorry I forgot to come yesterday.

EXERCISE 120.   Intermediate and Advanced

Note: **Statements.** (See Exercises 118 and 119.)

Must in Reported Speech. We use "must" sometimes as a true present tense, sometimes as a future. It is usually changed accordingly in Reported Speech. We also use "must" in rules and regulations: this behaves like any expression of universal truth or an obvious natural law; that is, it doesn't change when put into Reported Speech.

1. "Must" as a true present will change to past.
(a) I must go now. (*He said he had to go at once.*)
(b) I needn't go yet. (*He said he didn't have to go.*)
(c) I mustn't go there. (*He said he wasn't to go there.*)

2. "Must" as future (= *shall have to*) changes to "should/ would".

(a) I must go again next week. (*He said he would have to go ...*)

(b) I needn't go again next week. (*He said he wouldn't have to go ...*)

(c) I mustn't, etc. (*as for* 1 (c) *above*).

3. "Must" as a rule or regulation, or with the meaning "it is clearly so", does not change. (Nor do other similar general truths.)

(a) You must always take your shoes off before entering a mosque.
   (*He pointed out that we must always take ...*)

(b) The earth moves round the sun.
   (*At school we learned that the earth moves ...*)

Put the following sentences into Reported Speech, introducing them with a verb in the past tense:

1. He is going to London tomorrow.
2. You must always write your homework in ink.
3. Water boils at 100° (degrees) centigrade. (*At school we learnt that ...*)
4. They went away last month.
5. They had to go away last month.
6. They will be coming back soon.
7. They must return to London next Tuesday.
8. I should do the same if I were in your place.

No. 8

9. I haven't had enough time to finish what I intended **to do.** I can do some more later on.
10. You must go home at once.
11. I'm sorry I can't finish it at once, but I expect I can do it next week.
12. We needn't come to school next Monday, because we are having a holiday.
13. You mustn't cross the road against the red light.
14. We needn't get up so early every day.
15. You must do your homework again before Monday, though I must admit it is the first bad one you have done. You'll all get a new homework to do when you've finished it. (*Our teacher told us that ...*)

EXERCISE 121. Elementary

Note: Questions (with question-words).

Except when the question-word itself is the subject (*who? what? which?*), the subject and verb (or helping verb) change places in a direct question.

"*You are* late." "Why *are you* late?" (inversion)
"I *will help* you." "Who *will help* you?" (no inversion)

In *reported questions* there is no such inversion. The word-order remains as for a statement.

"*You are* late." ("Why *are you* late?")
He asked me why *I was* late.

"He *has been* in England." ("Where *has he* been?")
I asked where *he had* been.

(A very few idiomatic expressions remain as fixed patterns and do not change their word-order. The most important is "What is the matter?" There is no statement form of this question, so in Reported Speech we usually find *He asked me what was the matter* instead of the expected *He asked me what the matter was.*)

The question-word itself always remains in Reported Speech.

The following are common verbs that introduce Reported Questions: *ask, enquire, wonder, want to know.*

The same tense-changes, *etc.*, are made as for statements when the introducing verb is in Past time.

Put the following into Reported Speech with the introducing verbs in the **past tense**:

1. Where are you going?   (He asked me ...)
2. How did you do that?   (They wanted to know ...)
3. Who will come to the pictures with me?
4. Why are you so sad?
5. What is the matter?
6. Which book are you taking?   *I said which book*
7. Who showed you my work?   *I was taking.*
8. When did they tell you that?
9. Why has she not eaten anything?   *She hadn't eaten anything*
10. What is the time?   *was the time.*
11. How do you know that?
12. Where has he put my pencil?
13. When are you beginning your holiday?
14. How do you like this cake?
15. Why does he sing so loudly?   (We wondered ...)

EXERCISE 122.   Elementary

Note: **Questions** (by inversion).

Questions made by putting the verb (helping verb) before the subject (sometimes called *Yes/No* questions) require the word *whether* or *if* to join them to the introducing verb.

The word-order (as in the previous exercise) becomes that of an ordinary statement, and there are the usual tense-changes if the introducing verb is in the past tense.

"Have you seen John?"
He asked if (whether) *I had* seen John.

"Do you want a new book?"
He enquired whether (if) *I wanted* a new book.

Put the following sentences into Reported Speech, with the introducing verb in the **past tense**:

1. Are you enjoying yourself?   *I was enjoying yourself*
2. Did you see the match yesterday?   *if I saw the match*
3. Have you seen my new hat?
4. Do I look all right?   *if he looked all right*

No. 5

5. Are the grapes sour?
6. Is it time to go?
7. Will the taxi be here at eight o'clock?
8. Can you hear a noise?
9. Are my shoes cleaned yet?
10. May I use your telephone?
11. Is it raining very heavily?
12. Do you sleep in the afternoons?
13. Must the door be kept shut?
14. Was the train very full?
15. Have the children put away their toys?
16. Have you finished writing?
17. Need we come again next week?
18. Did you answer all the questions?
19. Can you understand me?
20. Will they let us know tomorrow?

EXERCISE 123. Elementary and Intermediate

Note: **Shall I/we?** (in Reported Questions).

Questions beginning "Shall I ... ?" are of two kinds.

1. **Pure Future Time.**

 Shall I ever know the answer?
 Shall we like our new teacher?

These change to *will/would* and 3rd person when reported:

 He wondered if he would ever know the answer.
 They wondered if they would like their new teacher.

2. **Request.**

 Shall I open the window?
 Shall we give out the books?

These remain *shall/should* for the 3rd person when reported:

 He asked if he should open the window.
 The pupils asked if they should give out the books.

Put the following questions into Reported Speech:

1. Shall I do it before tomorrow? (He asked ...)
2. Shall I call for you? (He asked ...)
3. Shall I like the concert? (He wondered ...)
4. Shall I leave it in the car? (He asked me ...)
5. Shall I live to be a hundred? (He wondered ...)
6. Shall I lay the table now? (She wanted to know ...)
7. Shall we buy your father a present? (They wondered ...)
8. Shall we know the answer tomorrow?
9. Shall I write it again? (She asked ...)
10. Shall I remember your name next time? (He wondered ...)
11. Shall we succeed in our examinations? (They wondered ...)
12. Shall I be in your way?
13. Shall I help you pack?
14. Shall I ask the little boy how to get there?
15. Shall we have time to finish? (They wondered ...)
16. Shall I be able to hear what he is saying?
17. Shall I hurry on and get the tickets?
18. Shall we wait till the others come? (They wanted to know ...)

19. Shall we require new books next time? (They wondered ...)
20. Shall I send it to you by post?

EXERCISE 124. Intermediate and Advanced

Note: **Reported Questions** (revision).

Try to use different introducing verbs, especially where there are double questions in this exercise.

Put the following questions into Reported Speech after a Past Tense introducing verb:

1. Where do you live?
2. Have you been to town today?
3. Where shall I be tomorrow?
4. Can you tell me where I can find the lecture-hall?
5. Where are you going?
6. Where did I leave my shirt and trousers?
7. Do you speak Russian? Do you think you can learn it in a year?
8. Can you lend me five pounds? Do you think you can trust me?
9. Do you know the way to the station?
10. How old is he now? Can he read yet?
11. Have you brought your books with you or not?
12. Why didn't you get up earlier?
13. What do you mean? Do you think I'm mad?
14. Are you American or do you come from Africa?
15. Must we be here by six or can we come a little later?
16. When will you come again? Shall I be seeing you next week?
17. How far is it to the National Theatre? Can I walk it in ten minutes or must I take a tram?
18. Can you count backwards from twenty in English? Shall I show you how to do it?
19. Where shall I meet you tomorrow? Shall I remember which bus to take?
20. Where are you from? Have you always lived in that place?

EXERCISE 125. Mainly Intermediate

Note: **Statements and Questions mixed** (in Reported Speech).

It is not normally necessary to repeat the introducing verb before every sentence in a passage of Reported Speech; shorter remarks can be joined with "and" or "but".

"I'm a student. I live in London and am studying English."
He said (that) he was a student, lived in London and was studying English.

If, however, the passage consists of statements mixed with questions, they can still be joined with "and" or "but", but the introducing verb must be changed each time.

"I'm a student. Are you a teacher?"
He said (that) he was a student *and asked* if I was a teacher.

If the order is **Question plus Statement** a useful phrase to use is *"adding that"*.

"Are you a teacher? I'm a student."
He asked if I was a teacher, adding that he was a student.

Useful introducing verbs are:

For statements only: tell, say, explain, remark.
For questions only: ask, wonder, enquire, want to know.

Put the following into Reported Speech, with the introducing verbs in the Past Tense:

1. It is cold in here. Is the window open?
2. Do you think it will rain? It is very cloudy.
3. I must write some letters now. What date is it?
4. What time is it? My watch has stopped.
5. This is a most interesting book. Have you ever read it?
6. What is the matter? You don't look very well.
7. That looks difficult to do. Can I help you?
8. Are you free tomorrow night? I'd like you to come to my party.
9. The dog has stolen the meat. What are we to do?
10. Who do you think is England's greatest dramatist? I like Shaw best.
11. How long have you been learning English? Your accent is very good.

12. It is time to go. Have you got all your things?
13. Would you like to see the garden? It is very pleasant out there.
14. You are late home. What have you been doing?

No. 14

15. I am learning English. Can you speak English?
16. Do you understand it now? I'll explain it again if you don't.
17. I've read this book before. Have you something else I can read?
18. May I take an apple? They look so nice.
19. Can you tell me the time? I shall have to leave at five.
20. Last year I visited Stratford-on-Avon. Have you ever been there? The town itself is delightful. Everywhere you come upon memories of Shakespeare's times, and (best of all) you can enjoy the living Shakespeare at the Memorial Theatre. I saw a fine production of "King Lear" there. Have you ever seen it performed? I saw three other plays as well, but "King Lear" impressed me the most.

Section 19

PASSIVE VOICE

EXERCISE 126. Elementary and Intermediate

Note: **General Remarks:** The passive voice of any transitive verb is made by combining its past participle with the appropriate tense of the verb *"to be"*.

He was/seen   (*past*)
They had been/warned   (*past perfect*)
We are being/watched   (*present continuous*)

The *passive voice* is used instead of the *active voice* when the speaker is mainly interested in the predicate (verb and object). The *subject* of his thoughts happens to be the grammatical *object*; his special interest in this part of the sentence makes him put it first because in the active voice his subject would have little interest or importance for him.

People play football everywhere.

(The speaker of this sentence is not really interested in his anonymous subject *people*; he is much more interested in *the playing of football*. So his thought is better and more strongly expressed by making his *mental* subject his *grammatical* subject, thus turning the sentence upside-down.) **Football is played everywhere.**

They haven't cleaned the blackboard.
The blackboard hasn't been cleaned.

One drinks a lot of tea in England.
A lot of tea is drunk in England.

Notice that in this kind of sentence, the original subject of the active voice disappears in the passive voice. It is quite unimportant, and the sentence is now complete without it. Most passive voice sentences in English have lost the original active voice subject because it isn't necessary. The real purpose of the passive voice is to bring the much more interesting predicate of the sentence to the front, because this is the most important part of the sentence in English.

Complete the following passive voice sentences in the tenses suggested:

1. This quarrel (forget) in a few years' time. (*Fut.*)
2. English (speak) all over the world. (*Pres.*)
3. These books mustn't (take) away. (*Infin.*)
4. My fountain-pen (steal). (*Pres. Perf.*)
5. He never (beat) at tennis (*Pres. Perf.*)
6. Your homework must (write) in ink. (*Inf.*)
7. A pupil (praise) when he works hard. (*Pres.*)
8. The books (lose) in the post. (*Past.*)
9. Books and pencils must (leave) on your desks. (*Inf.*)
10. Not a sound (hear). (*Past*)
11. These matches (make) in Sweden. (*Past*)
12. What (do) about this? (*Pres. Perf.*)
13. His new book (publish) next month. (*Fut.*)
14. Milk (use) for making butter and cheese. (*Pres.*)
15. The dog (leave) in the garden. (*Past.*)
16. Some ink (spill) on the carpet. (*Pres. Perf.*)
17. You (take) to see the old mosque tomorrow. (*Fut.*)
18. My other shoes (mend). (*Pres. Contin.*)
19. All your exam. papers (collect) at the end of the hour. (*Fut.*)
20. All our books (keep) in the cupboard. (*Pres.*).

EXERCISE 127. Intermediate

Note: **Verbs with two objects in Passive Voice.** About 40 fairly common verbs have two objects, a *direct* object (usually a thing) and an *indirect* object (usually a person). If the direct object is placed before the indirect, they are joined by the preposition "to" (occasionally "for").

> He gave a book to his brother.
> He bought a present for his friend.

If the indirect object is placed first, no preposition is needed to join them.

> He gave his brother a book.
> He bought his friend a present.

It usually does not matter which of the two objects is placed first; but if one of them is much longer or more emphatic than the other, it is usually placed last. For this reason the indirect object almost always comes first when it is a pronoun.

He gave a book to the young man who had just come in.
He bought me a book about tenth-century Arabian scholars.

In the Passive Voice it is more usual to make the *Indirect Object* the subject of the Passive (perhaps because we have a greater interest in persons than things). If the Direct Object is of special interest, it can also become the subject of the Passive Voice, the preposition "to" (or "for") being retained.

John was given a book for his birthday.
This fine new bicycle was given to John for his birthday.

The Passive pattern *John was given a book* is rare with the verbs *take*, *read* and *write*; it is only found commonly with *read* and *write* when no *direct object* is included.

I've never been written to like this before.

Put the following sentences into the passive voice, using the indirect objects (in bold type) as subjects:

1. People gave **the queen** a warm welcome.
2. People will show **her** the new buildings.
3. Someone has already paid **the carpenter** for mending the chair.
4. They promised **the boys** a prize if they passed the exam.
5. Somebody will tell **the passengers** what time the train leaves.
6. The doctor ordered **me** to stay in bed.
7. Someone lent **them** a boat for the afternoon.
8. Someone taught **him** French and gave **him** a dictionary.
9. They offered **us** a bigger house at a cheaper rent.
10. They fetched something to drink for **the speaker**.
11. They will ask **you** several questions.
12. When we first met, they had already offered **me** a job at the bank.
13. They bought **the children** an ice-cream each.
14. Someone asked **both boys** to leave the garden.
15. They've sent **us** the same book as they sent **us** last week.

16.   They offered **my father** a post as manager.
17.   They will allow **us** five minutes' break between lessons.
18.   People have asked **us** to be there at eight o'clock.
19.   They told the **new students** where to sit.
20.   Someone is showing **her** how to do it.

EXERCISE 128.   Intermediate

Note: Sometimes the active voice subject is important or interesting enough to be necessary in the passive voice form of the sentence. If so, it is usually introduced with the preposition "by".
The town was destroyed by an earthquake.
(In these exercises we shall add the word "agent" to sentences that require the original subject to be retained in the passive voice in this way.)
Verbs that require prepositions (laugh *at*, look *at*, speak *to*, etc.), or adverb particles (look *up* a word, put *on* and take *off* clothes, *etc.*), need some care when we use them in the passive. It is very easy for a student to leave out these small words, which will now come at the end of the phrase.

They will look after you well.
You will be well looked after.

When one has looked up all the words,...
When all the words have been looked up, ...

Put the following sentences into the passive voice, using the word in **bold type** *as the subject where this is indicated:*

1.   People asked John where he had been.
2.   Someone showed **the visitors** into the best room.
3.   People speak well[1] of **him**.
4.   Someone must look into this matter.
5.   They told her to be quick.
6.   They punished me for something I didn't do.
7.   Has anybody answered your question?
8.   Someone has cooked this fish excellently.
9.   You must write examination papers in ink.
10.   They fought a battle here 200 years ago.

[1] It is usual to put an adverb of manner immediately in front of the past participle it qualifies in the Passive Voice. E.g., *Your last homework was very badly written.*

11. Somebody has pushed the table into a corner.
12. Someone reads to the old blind lady every evening.
13. People told them to wait outside.
14. Someone gave **my sister** a box of chocolates for her birthday.
15. They gave **the best present** to the poorest child of all.
16. Nobody has slept in that room for years.
17. They gave me ten pence change at the shop.
18. She will look after the little girl well.
19. A car ran over our dog. (*Agent*)
20. The teacher promised **Mary** a prize if she worked well.
21. Somebody must finish this work.
22. Shakespeare wrote this sonnet. (*Agent*)
23. Someone gave out the news on the radio this morning.
24. The clock stopped because someone didn't wind it up.
25. Somebody carried the little boy up to bed.
26. Someone has brought this child up very badly.
27. People often ask **a policeman** the way.
28. Why didn't they tell **me** the truth about this?
29. Nobody has answered my question properly.
30. An unseen hand opened the window. (*Agent*)

EXERCISE 129. Intermediate and Advanced

Note: **More difficult sentences in the Passive Voice.** (See notes to Ex. 128.)

"People say" = "it is said"

The passive form *it is said* is no better than *people say*, because it also has a vague subject, the introductory *it*. A stronger way of expressing this idea is to make the subject of the clause introduced by "it" the subject of the Passive Voice.

People say that figs are better for us than bananas.
It is said that figs are ...
Figs are said to be better for us than bananas.

Reflexive Passive.

When the same person is both subject and object in the Active Voice, a reflexive pronoun is used in the Passive Voice. This is very common with "let".

F

Don't let people hear you.   (2nd person)
Don't let yourself be heard.   (or "*yourselves*")

He let people cheat him.   (3rd person)
He let himself be cheated.

*Put the following sentences into the passive voice, **using the** word in **bold type** as your subject where this is indicated:*

1. We oughtn't to speak about such things in class.
2. They will send him to school on Monday.
3. People should make lessons more interesting **for children.**
4. Someone left the light on all night.
5. His brother just beat John in the high-jump. (*Agent*)
6. Has anyone mended that chair yet?
7. Nobody has ever spoken to me like that before!
8. A friend lent **me** this book. (*Agent*).
9. They've asked some friends of hers to join us.
10. Didn't they tell the pupils to be here by three o'clock?
11. I'd like someone to read to me. (*Passive infin.*)
12. No one has drunk out of this glass.
13. The fire destroyed many valuable paintings. (*Agent*)
14. We ate up all the biscuits yesterday.
15. People will laugh at **you** if you wear a hat like that.

No. 15

16. The same man mended your shoes. (*Agent*)
17. People were carrying the chairs out into the garden.
18. I hate people looking at me. (*Passive gerund*)
19. People shan't speak to me as if I were a child.

20. Someone has locked the box and we can't open it. (*Two passives*)
21. Did the noise frighten you? (*Agent*)
22. Someone has found the boy the people wanted. (*Two passives; put relative clause inside main clause.*)
23. Don't let the others see you. (*Reflexive*)
24. Did nobody ever teach you how to behave?
25. People did nothing until he came.
26. One cannot eat an orange if nobody has peeled it. (*Two passives*)
27. You must account for every penny.
28. Somebody can't have shut the box properly.
29. People say that **tortoises** live longer than elephants.
30. I should love someone to take me to the circus.
31. His grandmother brought him up, and he got his education in Paris. (*Two passives*)
32. They must have given **you** the paper that they meant for the advanced students. (*Two passives*)
33. It surprised me to hear that someone had broken into your house. (*Two passives*)
34. People must leave everything as it is and lock the room up. (*Two passives*)
35. We haven't moved anything since they sent you away to cure you. (*Three passives*)
36. No-one has ever taken me for an Englishman before, though someone *did* once speak to me as if I were an American. (*Two passives*)
37. I've only used this pen once since the day I had it mended. (*Two passives*)
38. Naturally one expects you to interest yourself in the football team (that) they have put you into. (*Three passives*)
39. People generally assume that money brings happiness. (Money ...)
40. When I was very little, people used to read to **me** out of a book of fairy-tales that someone had given me for my birthday. (*Two passives*)

Section 20

MISCELLANEOUS

EXERCISE 130.   Elementary and Intermediate

Note: **Much (many), far, long.**

These words are seldom used in affirmative sentences, unless further modified, e.g. by *very*, or *too*. They are generally replaced by the following compound forms.

Much: *a lot (of), a great deal (of), a large amount (of), plenty (of)*—more colloquial, *lots (of)*.

Many: *a lot (of), a large number (of), plenty (of)*—more colloquial, *lots (of)*.

Many is less objectionable than *much* in affirmative sentences. Both are possible as active subjects or after "there is", *etc.* (mainly as pronouns).

Far (off, back, etc.): *a long way* (off, back, *etc.*).

Long: *a long time.*

Examples of the above remarks:
   You have put *a lot of* sugar in my tea.
   You have put *too much* sugar in my tea.
   You have*n't* put *much* sugar in my tea.
   There is much to be said for the habit of drinking tea.
   I bought *a lot of* books in London.
   Did you read much last winter?
   Did you read many books last winter?
   There are many books to choose from.
   It is*n't far* to school from here.
   It's *a long way* to my house from here.
   Have you been waiting *long*?
   We had to wait *a long time* for an answer.

Read the following statements in the affirmative:

1. He hasn't got much money.
2. It wasn't far off.

3. You haven't done much.
4. She hasn't given me much.
5. We haven't gone far.
6. He hasn't got much work to do.
7. I have not invited many people to my party.
8. You haven't had much to eat.
9. They don't live far off.
10. It is not far to the police station.
11. We haven't walked far today.
12. You haven't got much time.
13. I have not heard much about it.
14. There are not many trees in the garden.
15. His house is not far from mine.
16. It wasn't far back, was it?
17. You haven't got much to do, have you?
18. The sea is certainly not far off.
19. You haven't been gone long.
20. I have not bought many apples.
21. London is not very far from Liverpool.
22. You were not far away when it happened.
23. We hadn't long to wait.
24. The children don't make much noise.
25. He doesn't live far out, does he?

EXERCISE 131. Elementary

Note: **The Comparison Game.**

By asking first *How is X like Y?* then *How does X differ from Y?* we can practise the making of simple sentences on a simple practical theme. The following list of word-pairs can be used for X and Y.

Elementary example: CHAIR/TABLE.

1. **How is a chair like a table?**
    They are (both usually) made of wood.
    They (usually) have four legs.
    We find them in a house (dining-room, café, *etc.*).
    They are both pieces of furniture. (*etc., etc.*)

2. **How does a chair differ from a table?**
A chair has a back.
We sit *on* a chair; *at* a table.
We *sit* on a chair, *write* on a table.
A table is (usually) larger than a chair.   (*etc., etc.*)

Do not spend too long with any one pair of words, and do not try to invent sentences that are too difficult; pupils will need help in finding the right words now and then.

Using the following pairs of words, make a few simple sentences on the two questions:

(a) **How is X like Y?**
(b) **How does X differ from Y?**

PEN/PENCIL	GLASS/CUP
HOUSE/FLAT	DRESS/SUIT
ORANGE/APPLE	CAR/BUS
COW/SHEEP	HORSE/DOG
BUTCHER/BAKER	ARM/LEG
TENNIS/FOOTBALL	CIGAR/CIGARETTE
SOLDIER/SAILOR	BUTTER/CHEESE
CHICKEN/DUCK	TEA/COFFEE
ICE/SNOW	DOOR/WINDOW
TEXTBOOK/NOTEBOOK	DOCTOR/DENTIST
CHAIR/SOFA	TRAM/TRAIN

EXERCISE 132.   Intermediate and Advanced

Note: **More difficult examples.**   (See previous exercise.)

GATE/DOOR	SHOES/SLIPPERS
SALT/PEPPER	CINEMA/THEATRE
ROAD/STREET	CHURCH/MOSQUE
FRUIT/VEGETABLE	CHESS KING/CHESS
UMBRELLA/SUNSHADE	QUEEN
TRAM-DRIVER/TRAM-	VIOLIN/TRUMPET
CONDUCTOR	CELLAR/ATTIC
NAIL/SCREW	CUPBOARD/WARD-
BEARD/MOUSTACHE	ROBE
POSTMAN/POLICEMAN	LETTER/POSTCARD

SPOON/FORK	POETRY/PROSE
BOXING/WRESTLING	SILK/WOOL
RIVER/CANAL	FLOOR/CEILING
CUSHION/PILLOW	SOUP/ICE-CREAM
STAIRS/STEPS	CLOCK/WATCH

Section 21

PREPOSITIONS AND ADVERBIAL PARTICLES

EXERCISE 133.   Elementary and Intermediate

Note: **Prepositions.**

These are usually put before the words they control; they show relations of different kinds, the commonest being of space (position, direction, *etc.*), time, and various mental attitudes.

Prepositions can also come *after* the words they govern, especially in questions and relative or interrogative clauses.

Examples:

Is this the book (that) it is in?

That's the man I gave it to.

Many verbs are strongly associated with certain prepositions. They can be conveniently grouped into two classes:

(*a*)   with meaning that is clear from that of the verb itself.

(*b*)   with an idiomatic meaning.

Examples:

(*a*)   Take it off the chair and put it on the table.

He is sitting at the window that looks on to the garden.

He spoke about his holidays.

(*Notice a very similar sentence of another pattern:* He spoke about twenty minutes. *Here the prepositional phrase is an adverb of time, whereas in the other example it joins the verb mentally to "holidays".*)

(*b*)   John takes after his father.   (resembles)

His mother looks after him.   (cares for)

The ship was making for the harbour.   (going towards)

We're looking forward to your visit.   (awaiting with pleasure)

There is no space in this book for detailed work on prepositions and adverbial particles; information on this can be found in any good course, and also in H. E. Palmer's "Grammar of English Words" (Longmans) or "The Advanced Learner's Dictionary" (O.U.P.). The following two lists contain the most important prepositions; those in the first list are essential, and should be known to any student of English in the first two years of study.

List 1.   about, after, along, among, at, before, behind, between, by, down, for, from, in, in front of, into, like, near, next to, of, off, on, out of, over, past, round, since, through, till (until), to (towards), under, up, with, without.

List 2.   above, across, against, below, beside, beyond, concerning. despite, except, inside, in spite of, opposite, outside.

Put in suitable prepositions:

1. I go ... school every day.
2. My sister stays ... home.
3. The train arrived ... Waterloo ... 6 p.m.
4. Meet me ... noon ... Thursday.
5. I haven't seen you ... a week.
6. I have been away ... Saturday.
7. *Hamlet* was written ... Shakespeare.
8. I was born ... London, but now I live ... Lynton, a small village ... Devonshire.
9. Cats like to sit ... the roof.

No. 9

10. Write ... pencil.
11. They went home ... foot.
12. I like to go ... the country ... car.
13. Get ... the tram here, and get out ... the third stop.
14. There are many bridges ... the Thames.
15. I bought this hat ... fifty pence.
16. The train left here ... Paris ... midnight.
17. This is a secret ... you and me.
18. What are you talking ...?
19. A man ... a red beard went ... our house just now.
20. Wait ... me! Don't go ... me!
21. The teacher sits ... a desk ... the class.
22. ... him is a blackboard.
23. He walked ... the door, but fell ... a chair ... the way ... the room.
24. She sat ... her aunt and uncle.
25. We walked ... the hill ... the wood... the top.
26. I looked ... the window ... the busy street.
27. Go ... this street, turn right ... the post office, and then take the second turning ... the left.
28. Count ... one ... ten ... your fingers!
29. It is best to draw lines ... a ruler.
30. Can you push it ... the keyhole or ... the door?
31. I would give it ... you ... pleasure if it were mine.
32. Is it far ... here ... the station?
33. No; it takes five minutes ... bus, or you can walk it ... a quarter of an hour.
34. The house is ... fire! Call ... help!
35. Will you come ... me ... a swim ... the new swimming-pool ... lunch?
36. What are you laughing ... ?
37. She fell ... the stairs and knocked her glasses ... her nose.
38. I am looking ... a letter I had ... Sheila this morning.
39. Will you be ... home ... six and seven o'clock tonight?
40. He is going for a trip ... the world ... July.
41. She fell ... the ladder when she was trying to pin ... a map.

42. The children often throw their ball ... the wall ... mistake.
43. Switzerland lies ... France, Germany and Italy.
44. He lives ... his parents not far ... here.
45. Don't be angry ... me, but listen ... what I have to say.
46. Who does that watch belong ... ?
47. Children ... four years ... age do not often go ... school.
48. Britain was invaded ... William the Conqueror ... 1066.
49. I love to sit ... the trees ... the shade.
50. What were you talking ... him ... ?

EXERCISE 134. Elementary and Intermediate

Note: **Adverbial Particles.**

Most of these have the same form as corresponding prepositions. The following seven are adverbial particles only (*i.e.* never used as prepositions).

> away, back, out; backward(s), downward(s), forward(s), upward(s).
> They are mainly found as part of **compound verbs** (sometimes called **phrasal verbs**). These verbs are of two kinds:

(a) With literal meaning of the two parts (*e.g.* go in/pay back/take off/put on/walk away/come out, *etc.*).

(b) with idiomatic meaning of the two parts (*e.g.* keep on (*continue*), blow up (*explode*), bring about (*cause*), back up (*support*), give in (*yield*), *etc.*).

Some of the (a) compounds can be followed by a preposition, making a new combination with an idiomatic meaning (*e.g.* go in for (*enjoy by practising*), come out with (*say suddenly*), put up with (*bear, suffer*), *etc.*).

> A foreign student does not always find it easy to distinguish between the idiomatic use of a verb followed by a preposition and a true Phrasal Verb compound made with an adverb particle. He merely *looks upon* (prep.) these little words as annoying mysteries and *looks up* (adv.) their meaning in a dictionary. Here are the chief differences:

A preposition belongs to and goes closely with the **(pro)noun** it governs:

He laughed/at the boys.

He spoke/to them; he spoke/about his adventures.

He stayed/at home; and looked/out of the window.

An adverb particle is closely tied to the *verb* as part of a new compound; as if joined to it by a hyphen:

He looked-up/the word in a dictionary.

They blew-up/the bridge, and the rebels gave-in.

WORD-ORDER.

The **preposition** must precede its (pro)noun object (but see also note to Ex. 133. para. 2).

The **adverb particle** can come either before or after the object of the sentence, unless this object is a long one; it is always placed *after* a pronoun.

Look up the word in the index[1] *or*

Look the word up in the index!

Look **it up** in the index!

Compare this with "up" *as a preposition:*

Look up the chimney! (*no alternative word-order*)

Look **up it**!

Here is another pair:

He couldn't get across the river; ... get across it. (*prep.*)

He couldn't get his speech across; ... get it across. (*adv.*)

(= to succeed in communicating)

STRESS.

At the end of a phrase, a *verb with preposition* has a falling stress on the **verb**:

Who does he ˋtake after?

Give it to the man you ˋspoke to.

At the end of a phrase, a *verb with adverb particle* (Phrasal Verb) has a falling stress on the **adverb**:

It was a hard word to look ˋup.

This is the book he brought ˋback, and here's the one he wants to take ˋout.

[1] *We must use this word-order with long objects:*
Look up all the difficult words and phrases in the index!

Verbs with adverb particles and prepositions in this position behave like Phrasal Verbs, too:

> He has a lot to put 'up with.
> Chess is a good game to go 'in for.

Put in suitable prepositions or adverbial particles:

1. Put ... your hat and come ... for a walk.
2. Don't look ... Someone is following us close ...
3. Look ... Mary! She has got a new dress ...
4. ... what time do you get ... ... the morning?
5. You will catch cold if you go ... ... the rain ... a hat.
6. When you go ... town, please bring ... a pot ... jam ... me.
7. Please pick ... that piece ... paper ... the floor.
8. It would be good ... us to wake ... early ... the morning and take a walk ... the garden.
9. We must choose ... a holiday ... country and one ... the sea.
10. I am ringing you ... to ask if you will come ... ... a walk ... dinner.
11. The aeroplane will take ... ... six o'clock.
12. We are ... war ... them.
13. When you grow ... you will be able to stay ... late, but not ... then.

No. 13

14. Why don't you put ... the light, or do you prefer to sit ... the dark?
15. Some animals sleep ... day and wake up ... night.
16. We used to live ... a house ... the river.
17. Don't give this coat ..., you could sell it ... quite a lot ... money.
18. She should look ... the baby better, even if she doesn't care ... it.
19. I must send ... the doctor; he will soon find ... what is wrong ... him.
20. Have you any money ... you?
21. We walked ... miles ... fields ... corn.
22. I'm just going ... the corner to post a letter. I'll be ... ... a few minutes.
23. I prefer beef ... mutton.
24. I am going to tear ... all my old letters ... lunch.
25. We all stayed ... the party till it was ... three o'clock, ... my sister, who went home ... midnight.
26. I took a book ... politics ... ... the library, and began to turn ... the pages.
27. The enemy took ... positions immediately ... ours.
28. If you sit ... me, I can watch how you do it.
29. It is unlucky to wear your socks ... ...
30. Don't swim ... the buoy; there are dangerous currents here.

EXERCISE 135. Intermediate and Advanced

Note: More difficult examples of prepositions or adverbial particles.

Add the missing prepositions or adverbial particles:

1. I came ... it quite ... chance as I was looking ... some old papers.
2. Lean it ... the wall if you don't want it to fall ...
3. Do you think there is enough food to go ... ?
4. I don't get ... very well ... him.
5. She has saved ... so much money she will be well ... ... the rest ... her life.

6. What do you think ... dividing it ... the rest ... them?

7. I don't like people who show ..., especially ... public.

8. We were ... a loss to know what you meant ... your remark.

9. I don't understand; what are you getting ... ?

10. I know her ... sight, but not to speak ...

11. In this play they take ... several famous people ... today.

12. The fire is ..., we have run ... ... coal, so we shall just have to make the best ... it.

13. He shook me ... the hand and helped me ... with my coat.

14. The notice says "Keep ... the grass." You'd better look ... ... case a park-keeper comes.

15. ... all his faults you must admit that he's easy to get ... ...; he's always ... a good temper.

16. Speak ..., I can't hear you. You let your voice die ... at the end of every sentence.

17. ... spite ... many difficulties, the show went ... very well.

18. Don't be ... such a hurry, I can't keep ... ... you.

19. You can rely ... me to stand ... you if you are ... trouble.

20. I don't know how to get ... touch ... Mrs. Green, she's not ... the 'phone.

21. If you paint the figures ... bright colours they will stand ... more clearly.

22. We set ... as soon as the old man pointed ... the way to us.

23. Make yourself ... home; help yourself ... anything you want ... waiting to be asked.

24. I could do ... a hot cup of tea, but they've run ... ... sugar.

25. I left my friend leaning ... the lamp-post ... a cigarette ... his lips.

26. Who is going to pay ... all this damage ... my car?

27. It is very rude to point ... people ... that way.

28. It is bad to laugh ... children ... their mistakes.
29. He poured the water ... the jug ... a glass.
30. They were already ... ... sight beyond the hill, so it was impossible to catch them ...

APPENDIX ON CLAUSES

This book has dealt with only one type of clause (the conditional) in some detail, but exercises on other kinds of subordinate clauses are found under appropriate headings. A few types, notably Cause, Purpose, Result and Concession, are not expressly treated. This appendix will give a practical outline of clauses and the conjunctions that introduce them. In keeping with the spirit of the rest of the book, exercises in this section will be constructive and not analytical.

GENERAL REMARKS

A clause takes its name from its function (i.e. a noun clause behaves like a noun, an adverb clause like an adverb, *etc.*).

Students who have to analyse English sentences should note that many conjunctions can introduce clauses of more than one type; in fact any one clause is sometimes to be interpreted differently in different sentences. For example, the clause *"when he left"* looks like an adverbial clause of time, as in the sentence "The others came **when he left**." But we could make it function quite differently:

Can you tell me when he left?	(Noun: object)
When he left is still a mystery.	(Noun: subject)
Do you remember the day when he left?	(Adjective)
How could he know the result when he left before the end?	(Cause)
They invited him again even when he left once without saying goodbye.	(Concession)

NOUN CLAUSES

A. The most usual form is the **object-clause of reported speech.** (See Exercises 118 to 125.)

The noun clause of a **reported question** can be preceded by a preposition.

It depends on what you want me for.

I am anxious about where he has gone.

It reminds me of when I first went to school.

Don't let's worry about whether we'll be in time.

(N.B. "If" cannot be used here when the interrogative clause is introduced by a preposition; we can use "whether" only.)

(See Exercise 121 for clauses with *what, who, which*, etc.)

Reported statements are introduced by "that", which is only rarely preceded by a preposition. The two principal ways of getting over this difficulty when a preposition is needed are:

1. Omit the preposition where possible.

Examples: proud of   *I am proud that you have won.*
          surprised at *He was surprised that I knew English.*
          sorry for   *We're sorry that you can't come.*

This pattern is possible with most other such expressions of feeling, such as: *Sure of, glad of, angry with, aware of, afraid of, grateful (thankful) for, anxious for*, etc. Many of them can be logically analysed as adverb clauses: e.g. the last two examples above could equally well be called clauses of reason—clauses answering the question "Why?"

A few prepositions may still be used before the conjunction "that", the most usual being "except" and "in".

Examples: I forgot everything except that I wanted to go home.

He takes after his father in that he is fond of music.

In this last sentence "in that" might be considered as a conjunction introducing an adverb clause of manner—a clause answering the question "How?" (See under ADVERB CLAUSES, Section D.)

Note the expression "I don't care (for)", which has two meanings:

I don't care for what she does.   (*I don't like*)
I don't care what she does.   (*I'm indifferent*)

2. Use an introductory "it", "this" or "the fact" before the conjunction "that".

Examples: You can depend on it that he won't be pleased.

We must allow for the fact that she doesn't hear well.

It all amounts to this, that you have been cheated.

I'll see to it that you get home all right.

B.   Noun clause as **subject.**

Examples: That he has gone for good is now quite certain.

What you want is a cup of tea.

(*A cup of tea is what you want.*)

Whoever finishes first gets a prize.

The first type above is better expressed with an introductory "it". *It is now quite certain that …*

Exercise I.   *Say these sentences in a more natural way, using "it" as the first word:*

1.   That you are late is a pity.
2.   How useful these sentences are is quite clear.
3.   That you have come early is a good thing.
4.   That you lost your way is unfortunate.
5.   Whether he will come at all is doubtful.
6.   Where he went or where he came from is still not known.
7.   That we shall leave without paying is quite out of the question.
8.   How he knew my name is a mystery to me.
9.   That we didn't get back before midnight is quite true.
10.   How tea is made is important for everyone to know.
11.   What you ought to say and how you ought to say it is difficult to suggest.
12.   That we haven't met somewhere before seems strange.

13. That such a person ever existed must first be proved.
14. When he is coming back hasn't yet been decided.
15. What you look like is not important, but how you behave (is).

(See also Exercises 114 to 116 on *it is* and *there is* (*are*), etc.)

ADVERB CLAUSES

A. Place

Chief conjunctions: *where* (and its derivatives); *as.*

Examples: Go where you like!
     Put it back where you found it!
     She shall have music wherever she goes.
        (*Children's rhyme*)
     Wherever (it was) possible, they camped for
        the night.
     It's on your right as you face the station.

B. Time

Chief conjunctions: *when* (and its derivatives), *as soon as* (*ever*), *as long as* (*ever*), *until* (*till*), *before, after, by the time, while* (*whilst*), *as, now* (*that*), *once, since;* and the compound forms *no sooner ... than; scarcely* (*hardly*) *... when* (*before*); *not long* (*an hour, a minute, far,* etc.) *... when* (*before*).

Examples:

Let me know when you've finished. (*Can also be Noun Clause.*)
Come back as soon as (ever) you can.
You can stay as long as (ever) you want to.
Wait till (until) the light changes to green.
Look before you leap.
After he had had supper he went to bed.
I'll have finished by the time you get back.
Shoes repaired while you wait.
I met him as he was coming out of school.
Now you (come to) mention it, I suppose we *must* have met
    somewhere before.
You'll find the way all right once you get to the station.
She hasn't written since she went away. (*Main verb always
    perfect tense.*)

[1]He had no sooner arrived than he demanded a meal.
[1]He had scarcely left the house before we missed the jewels.
They hadn't gone very far when they met an old man.

For Future Time sentences see Exercises 72 and 74.

Exercise II.   *Join each of the clauses in (A) to the appropriate clause of time or place in (B):*

	A	B
1.	Come again	as long as is necessary
2.	Wait	by the time they got back
3.	He went out again	just as he was ringing the bell
4.	They must go home	as soon as you can
5.	There was nothing left	after he had finished his dinner
6.	He repaired our shoes for us	every time I meet her
7.	I opened the door	since you went to live in London
8.	I haven't heard from you	the moment he spoke
9.	She asks after you	before they get too tired
10.	I knew who it was	while we waited.

C. Contrast

Certain conjunctions of place and time are now used to introduce a contrasting clause, very like the clauses of concession (*see section J below*).

Examples:

I wanted to go on, whereas my friend wanted to turn back.
Now there is nothing but desert, where there used to be a fertile plain.
At the same time that one side was disarming, the other was preparing for war.
While one half of the town was in ruins, the other half was almost intact.

D. Manner

Chief conjunctions: *as, how, in that.*

Examples: He did as I told him.

---

[1] Also with inversion: No sooner had he .... etc.

You may finish it how you like.

We were at a disadvantage in that they outnumbered us two to one.

The list is as follows.   (= *as it follows*)

The journey, as I recall it, was long and tedious.

Note on "like".

Except in formal English, "like" is commonly used in place of the conjunction "as". It is still frowned upon by purists, but has persisted in the popular language, as well as in the informal speech of those who would claim to know better, for centuries. The conjunction "as" serves many purposes, and is therefore a word of vague meaning; the earlier "like as" (= *in the same way as*) probably gave rise to the popular use of "like" by itself in clauses of that type as it is a word with a more distinctive meaning. For this reason we feel that sentences like the following are quite good English, despite the die-hard theorists:

She swims like I do; badly.

We don't use that form in English, like they do in French.

They may beat us again, like they did in 1950.

The stones bounced harmlessly off him like water (does) off a duck's back.

Sink like a stone (does); drink like a fish; run like a hare, *etc.* (These last may be considered as preposition phrases; 'in the manner of a stone', *etc.*, but it is logical to supply a verb, since it is the verb that is being compared.)

These sentences, though still not approved of in "examination English", are certainly acceptable informal English. Notice that in each case there is an implied repetition of the verb: "*X does something in the same way that Y does it.*" Where this condition does not hold, we feel that *"like"* cannot be used, even colloquially. In the following examples we can only use *"as"*:

I'll do as you tell me.

It's only half a mile, as the crow flies.

Don't trouble to change; come just as you are.

You'd better write as I suggest.

(*Compare this with:* Write it like (as) I do, in capital letters.)

Another kind of sentence we often meet is of the type:
I want a new silk dress like my friend Mary has.

It looks like a clause introduced by "like"; but can also be interpreted as a suppressed relative clause by adding "the one that" after "like".

E. Degree (positive, also extent or amount).

Chief conjunctions: *as; as ... as; not so (as) ... as.*

The subordinate clause compares something to the main clause in equal degree. The recommended distinction *"as good as* he is" and *"not so* good *as* he is" is not in fact strictly kept, probably because of the similar origins of "so" and "as". The form *"not as* good *as* he is" is quite acceptable English.

Examples:

Life is as pleasant as you make it.

Nothing is so (as) bad as you think it is.

Nothing upset me so much as that he had quite forgotten me.

(In this sentence "so" is stressed; "as" cannot take stress, and "so" is used when we want to emphasize the intensity of the degree by means of speech stress. It should not be confused with "so" introducing a result clause, as in section L.)

This morning I'm as well as (I have) ever (been).

Mend it as best you can. (= *as well as possible*)

F. Degree (proportionate, or parallel).

Chief conjunctions: *according as (to), in proportion as, the ... the.*

Examples:

The quicker we walk, the sooner we shall get there.

We shall get there earlier or later according as we walk quicker or slower.

You'll get paid (more or less) according to how you work.

A person isn't always paid according as he works.

    ... according to how he works.

    ... in proportion as he works.

    ... in proportion to how he works.

The more (we are together), the merrier (we shall be).

G. Degree (comparative).

   Chief conjunction: *than*.

   Examples:

She is much older than she looks.

We arrived sooner than we thought.

She was more clever than (she was) pretty.

This morning I'm better than (I have) ever (been).

In accordance with the tendency to avoid the nominative form when the pronoun is not obviously the subject of a verb immediately following, one commonly hears:

   You're better than me; he's happier than her, *etc.*

As a predicate after a verb of the "to be" type there is no real objection to using this disjunctive or separated pronoun form (like the French "lui", "moi", *etc.*), but students should note that it is still held to be a popular pattern not recommended for formal writing, and that it *must not be used with transitive verbs* for fear of confusion:

   I like her better than (I like) him.

   I like her better than you (do).

   (*See also Exercise* 13.)

H. Degree (restriction).

   Chief conjunctions: *as, so (as) long as, so (as) far as, in so far as, for all (anything) [that], (not) that.*

   Examples:

You can stay here, so long as you are quiet.

You can stay here, so (as) far as I'm concerned.

You can stay here, for all I know (care).

"Has he stayed here before?" "Not that I know of."

"Has he stayed here before?" "Not so far as I know."

I. Cause.

Chief conjunctions: *because, since, as, when, seeing (that); for.*

Examples:

I can't go, because I have no ticket.

Since we are early, let's have a drink first.

As you have been here before, you'd better lead the way.

We must finish now, for it's nearly bedtime.

You can't expect him to know the story when he hasn't read it.

You can't expect him to know the story seeing (that) he hasn't read it.

Note on: *for, since, as, because.*

For is really a co-ordinating conjunction, used to introduce a natural reason or obvious fact. It is included above because its meaning is approximately that of the subordinating conjunction *since.*

He is not allowed to smoke, for he is only a boy.

Since also implies that the reason is obvious or natural. A *since*-clause usually precedes the main clause; there is more interest in the main clause for the speaker or hearer than in the reason introduced by *since.*

Since he is only a boy, he is not allowed to smoke.

As also usually comes first in the sentence, and (like *since*) also throws the speaker's enphasis on to the main clause. The reason introduced by *as* is not necessarily obvious or natural, which it usually is with *for* or *since.*

As I'm very busy these days, I shan't be able to take my usual holiday.

Because seldom comes first in a sentence. There is more interest in the reason introduced by *because* than in the main clause.

I can't come just now, because I'm busy writing a book.

A common meaning of a clause beginning 'or else' is 'because otherwise'.

Come early, or else you won't find a seat.

(= *Come early, because you won't find a seat if you don't.*)

J. Concession (and contrast).

Chief conjunctions: *although, (even) though, (even) if, as, whoever,* etc., *no matter who (when,* etc.).

Examples:

(Al)though it is late, we'll stay a little longer.

Late though it is, we'll stay a little longer.

Bad as things are, we mustn't give up hope.

Even if (though) things *are* bad, we ...

However bad things are, we ...

No matter how bad things are, we ...

I shouldn't worry if he *has* forgotten you. (= *even though*)

I'll buy one whatever it costs (*may cost*).

K. Purpose.

Chief conjunctions: *that, in order that, so (that), lest, for fear (that), in case.*

The words "*may, might, shall, should*" commonly occur with the verb after these conjunctions. "*Might*" and "*should*" must be used when the verb of the main clause is in the past tense. "*That*" can be omitted wherever it occurs between brackets in this section.

Examples:

They rented the top-floor that they might have a good view. (*The simple "that"-clause is not much used to express purpose in modern English.*)

They have arrived early so that (in order that) they may (shall) not miss the overture. (*Literary style.*)

They've come early so (that) they won't miss the overture. (*Good spoken English style.*)

They arrived early so that (in order that) they might (should) not miss the overture. (*Literary style.*)

They came early so (that) they wouldn't miss the over-ture. (*Good spoken English style.*)

Make a note of it so (that) you don't (shan't) forget.

Make a note of it lest you (may, might, should) forget. (*Literary.*)

Make a note of it in case you forget. (*Good colloquial.*)

We didn't move lest we should (might) wake him up. (*Literary.*)

We didn't move for fear (that) we should (might) wake him up. (*Literary.*) (*" for fear (that)" is mainly used with a negative main clause*)

We didn't move in case we woke him up. (*Good colloquial.*)

L. Result.

Chief conjunctions: *that, so (that), so (such) ... that; but that* (negative).

"Result" clauses are like an inversion of clauses of cause. The "so that" introducing a clause of purpose can always be replaced by "in order that"; we cannot do this with "so that" introducing a clause of result. We can, however, reverse the clauses in such a sentence, changing the main clause into one of cause (introduced by "as", "since" or "because").

She bought a book so (that) she might learn English. (*Purpose.*)

She bought a book in order that she might learn English.

She bought a good book, so (that) she learnt English well. (*Result.*)

She bought so good a book that she learnt English well.

She bought such a good book that she learnt English well. (= *As she bought a good book, she learnt English well.*)

Notice that we sometimes find sentences that can be interpreted either way. In the spoken language the **Result** sentence would be heard with two phrases of **falling intonation**, the **Purpose** sentence with *rising intonation on the main clause*.

Purpose: I wrote clearly so (that) anyone could read it. (*in order that*)

· ＼ ＼／ | · · ＼ · · · · ·

Result : I wrote clearly, so (that) anyone could read it. (*because I wrote clearly*)

· — ＼ · | · · ＼ · · · · ·

Examples of clauses of result:

Are you deaf that you didn't hear me?

(= *Did you fail to hear me because you are deaf?*)

It was quite windy, so (that) we had to button our coats up.

We were so hungry (that) we couldn't wait for knives and forks.

It's such a good story (that) I'll never forget it.

It's so good a story (that) I'll never forget it. (*Literary*.)

I shall never be so tired but that (but what) I shall be able to write to you. (*Literary style only*.)

I shall never be so tired that I shan't be able to write to you.

It never rains but it pours. (*Old proverb*.)

(= Once it starts to rain, it rains hard: *Troubles multiply*).

Exercise III. *Complete the following sentences of purpose or result:*

1. He was so kind (that) ...
2. Come a little nearer so that ...
3. I'll give you some money in case ...
4. He ran so quickly (that) ...
5. They live such a long way away (that) ...
6. We mustn't make a noise for fear ...
7. He hurried back in order that ...
8. He didn't shout lest ...
9. She was so lazy (that) ...
10. I'm so tired (that) ...
11. (You'd) better buy one now in case ...
12. I've bought you some knitting needles so (that) ...
13. It was such a dull party (that) ...
14. He hid behind the door in order that ...
15. I didn't come any earlier for fear ...

Exercise IV. *Here are seven short sentences or clauses:*

1. Just sit where you like.
2. No, keep it as long as you wish.
3. Just do as I tell you.
4. Well, it's not so bad as I thought.
5. The earlier, the better.
6. In case it gets broken.
7. Well, fasten them like I do. (See note in section D.)

Use one of the above as a response to each of the remarks below:
(The teacher should make the remark, and the student choose one of the above seven phrases as a suitable response to it.)

1. Which is my place?
2. I expect you found a lot of mistakes in my homework.
3. Why are you wrapping the vase in a cloth?
4. Let's see if we can start before breakfast, shall we?
5. You don't mind my borrowing this, I hope?
6. That's a dull grammar you're reading, isn't it?
7. My skis are slipping.
8. Why do you keep your pen in your inside pocket?
9. My entrance ticket hasn't (got) a number on it.
10. Would you like me to bring the book back next week?
11. My papers won't stay in the folder.
12. What are you putting the microscope away for?
13. I hope I don't do anything to displease the visitors.
14. I hear you've hurt your finger badly.
15. What about leaving this dull party before the end?

M. Condition.
(See Exercises 78 to 84.)

Infinitive phrases, often a shorter way of expressing a clause, can be practised in Exercises 92 to 95.

ALPHABETICAL INDEX

(References are to exercises throughout)